❧ A Hand Upon the Time ❧

Charles Dickens was one of the greatest English novelists and the most popular writer of the nineteenth century. His experiences with people and with life around him were so intense and so vivid that he was able to capture it all in his writing in a way that no one else could.

When Dickens began to write his novels, he had behind him memories of a happy childhood, but also the knowledge of poverty and family disgrace, of hunger and hardship. His apprenticeship to the law brought him in contact with many of the odd quirks of human nature. His years in the Press Gallery of the House of Commons had shown him the machinery of government; his travels as a reporter during the parliamentary recesses had given him a clear picture of English provincial life. He had been wholeheartedly in love and had experienced the pain of rejection. He had read widely and his life then as always was enriched by many friendships. During his entire life, he carried on a constant crusade against social injustices of all kinds. And when he was buried in Westminster Abbey, not only England, but every nation in the civilized world mourned for him.

A Hand
Upon the Time
A Life of Charles Dickens

by Lettice Cooper

ILLUSTRATED WITH PRINTS AND PHOTOGRAPHS

Pantheon Books

PICTURE CREDITS

Brown Brothers
pps. 12, 87, 174
New York Public Library Picture Collection
Frontispiece, pps. 18, 41, 52, 153, 172
The Bettmann Archive
pps. 36, 44, 52, 65, 75, 95, 102, 104, 113,
120, 133, 145, 178

To leave one's hand upon the time, with one tender touch for the mass of toiling people that nothing could obliterate would be to lift oneself above the dust of all the Doges.

CHARLES DICKENS

⤙ A Hand Upon the Time ⤚

⤙ 1 ⤚

CHARLES John Huffham Dickens was born on February 7, 1812 in Landport, a suburb of Portsmouth, a big naval port on the southern coast of England. He was the eldest son of John and Elizabeth Dickens, who already had a two-year-old daughter, Fanny. In 1812, the year of Napoleon's retreat from Moscow, England was at war with France on land and sea.

John Dickens worked as a clerk in the Navy Pay Office. His father, William Dickens, had been a footman in the employ of Lord Blandford, and had married one of the housemaids, Elizabeth Ball, who after her husband's death became housekeeper at Crewe Hall to the Member of Parliament for Chester.

This meant that John Dickens had grown up against a background of great houses. His eyes were early dazzled by the spacious rooms, the elegant company, the lavish food and drink, the carriages and the servants in livery. As a result he never managed to adapt himself to the conditions of life as a clerk on a moderate salary, which at the time of his marriage was £200 a year, worth much more, of course, in those days, than now. John was a short, stout, lively, cheerful man, very fond of company, with a taste for good food and wine. Always pleased with the sound of his own voice, he loved to make a speech on any possible occasion.

John Dickens married Elizabeth Barrow, whose father, Charles, was a Conductor of Money or Accountant to the Navy Board. Unfortunately Charles Barrow was discovered to have conducted £5000 of Navy Board Money into his own pocket. He was obliged to flee the country to escape prosecution. His daughter, Elizabeth, showed her loyalty to her defaulting parent by calling her eldest son Charles. The name Huffham, which he later spelled Huffam, was given to him for his godfather, Huffham, a ship's-rigger and mastmaker who lived at Limehouse near the London Docks. Elizabeth Dickens was pretty, gentle, and affectionate, but not much more practical than her husband. She went to a dance the night before her eldest son was born. Some of his biographers have remarked that the lively, restless Charles Dickens was almost born dancing.

When Charles was a few months old his parents moved to Mile End Terrace in Portsea, another suburb of Portsmouth. They took a small neat terrace house, with a tiny patch of garden in front, which Charles was to remember all his life. Navy pay clerks had to go wherever the Admiralty sent them. In 1817 John

Dickens was assigned to London and three years later to the Dockyard at Chatham, an inland port on the Medway, a tributary of the River Thames. His salary was now £350 a year, not bad for those days, but the war was over, and the cost of living was rising. Six more children were born, and although two had died in infancy it was still a large family to feed, especially since John Dickens spent more than he could afford on wine and other luxuries. He was very soon in debt.

The six years spent at Chatham were for young Charles "a time to be remembered like a happy dream through all our after life." In spite of money worries home was an easy, cheerful place full of affection. John Dickens never saw a crisis until it was upon him. Through all the years at Chatham he kept his good spirits; he could always manage to afford a treat even if he could not pay the butcher. He enjoyed taking Charles and Fanny to the theater when they were very young.

But Charles hardly needed to go to the theater, so vivid and dramatic were the impressions he received from the ordinary life around him. He watched everyone and noticed everything. His father soon began to take him for long walks. They walked from Chatham to the larger Medway port of Rochester. There Charles gazed eagerly at the bustling life of the town, the coaches rolling into the Inn yard, the travelers in their caped coats and shawls stamping their feet to warm them while the hostlers hastily changed the horses, and the fresh postboys mounted them.

Charles stared at the ships and the market stalls, the

beggars and tramps and gypsies, at the discharged sol-
diers, who often had wooden legs or arms. Sometimes
he saw a great man's coach with its liveried servants and
outriders, or a traveling company of actors unloading
their scenery at the stage door of the theater. It was all
very interesting. The sharp-eyed little boy missed nothing and stored up all these early impressions in his mind.

Sometimes for a change his father took him for walks
in the Kent countryside. Once they walked past a big
house called Gad's Hill, and Charles said to his father
that he would like to live in it. John Dickens, who, whatever his failings, was not the man to discourage anybody's dream, told the child that he might live there one
day if he worked hard and were persevering. Even John
Dickens would surely have been surprised if he had
known that Charles was to buy Gad's Hill in another
thirty-five years.

Though active and full of life Charles was not strong;
he suffered from violent spasms of stomach pain which
prevented him from playing with other boys. His mother
first taught him to read, though lessons were often inter-
rupted by the arrival of a new baby. Soon Charles went
with his sister Fanny to a day school where he was happy
and did well. But no lesson was as interesting to him as a
discovery that he made for himself as soon as he could
read.

John Dickens, with his usual tendency to spend money
on what other people did not regard as necessities, had
acquired a collection of such important books as *Roderick Random, Peregrine Pickle, The Arabian Nights,*

Tom Jones, The Vicar of Wakefield, Robinson Crusoe, Don Quixote and others. Charles found all these lying in a dusty heap in the attic and devoured them. In his novel, *David Copperfield,* so much of which is based on the story of his own life, Charles Dickens later told about this wonderful experience. "From that blessed attic they came out, a glorious host, to keep me company." He could console himself in any trouble by acting one of his favorite characters from these books.

I have been Tom Jones (a child's Tom Jones, a harmless creature), for a week together. I have sustained my own idea of Roderick Random for a month at a stretch. I had a greedy relish for a few volumes of Voyages and Travels that were on the shelves. For days I can remember to have gone about with the centre piece from an old set of boot trees, the perfect realization of Captain Somebody of the British Navy, in danger of being beset by savages, and resolved to sell his life at a great price.

When I think of it, the picture always rises in my mind of a summer evening, the boys at play in the Church yard, I sitting on my bed and reading as if for life.

Charles' other great pleasure was to visit his godfather Huffham at Limehouse. There he was made much of and encouraged to sing his comic songs. There he began to absorb the life on the banks of London's great river that was to enrich several of his novels. On these visits the little boy piping his comic songs to an indulgent audience of boatbuilders and mastmakers tasted the delight in giving a public performance that was to remain with him all his life.

In 1822 John Dickens was transferred from Chatham Dockyard to Somerset House in London, then the headquarters of the Navy Board. He now had five children living, Fanny, Charles, Letitia, Frederic and Alfred. He also had a number of debts. To make a settlement with his creditors before leaving Chatham he was obliged to sell most of his furniture.

When the family moved to London in the Fall of that year they left Charles behind to finish his term at school. He came up alone in the stagecoach, Commodore. He always remembered the smell of damp straw, "in which I was packed like 'game carriage paid.' There was no other passenger, and I consumed my sandwiches in solitude and dreariness, and it rained hard all the way and I thought life sloppier than I expected to find it." So Charles arrived in London, just eleven years old, at the end of his carefree childhood, though he did not know it.

⌁ 2 ⌁

CHARLES, who had been so happy at Chatham, hated the
new house, which he later described as "a mean small
tenement with a wretched little back garden abutting
on a squalid court." It was in Bayham Street, Camden
Town, which at that time was a nest of slums.

He had supposed that he would go to another school
in London, but he found to his dismay that there was no
question of it. His father could not afford to pay for it;
besides, Charles, he remarked, had *been* to school. Now
until he was old enough to work he must help his mother
at home, clean the boots and look after the younger
children.

Charles liked learning and already had a very clear
idea of the value of education. He felt desperate. He
loved his sister Fanny dearly, but it was hard for him to
rejoice when she won a scholarship to the Royal Academy of Music. Here was a way out for her from the life

of poverty and ignorance which seemed to be closing in on him. He was at this time, as he later described the young David Copperfield, "a child of excellent abilities, with strong powers of observation, quick, eager, delicate, and soon hurt bodily and mentally."

John Dickens immediately began to get into debt again. Now Charles was always hearing talk about "The Deed." This was a document that his father was perpetually drawing up and altering to state the terms of his settlement with his creditors. Unfortunately the creditors wanted money, not documents, so a part of John Dickens' salary had to go to them every week, which meant that there was not enough left to keep the family.

They were short of furniture since John Dickens had been obliged to sell some to satisfy his Chatham creditors, but they now had to begin pawning whatever they could spare. Since his father was at work all day, it fell to Charles to negotiate with the pawnbrokers. There were plenty of these in a place like Camden. London in those days was a city of the very rich and the very poor. Many people had to take their small possessions to the pawnbrokers' shops to raise a few shillings on them, always hoping to redeem them later on but this was rarely the case.

Charles soon knew every shop in the district that carried the three gilt balls over the door. Before long he was on friendly terms with all the pawnbrokers, who were quite impressed with the sharp-witted little boy. One of them used to ask him to repeat a word or two of the Latin he had learned at school.

It was a bad day for Charles when he had to take his father's collection of novels to be pawned. He would have been in despair without them but he happened to make friends with the widow of an old bookseller who lent him her late husband's stock.

Elizabeth Dickens, anxious to help, suddenly conceived the idea of starting a girls' school. Charles' godfather, Mr. Huffham, had often dealt with ships arriving from India. Mrs. Dickens thought that he must meet the guardians of children sent home, who would want to find a good school for them. She borrowed some money from Huffham, rented part of a house in Gower Street, and ordered a brass plate to be printed for the door with the words: "Mrs. Dickens' Establishment."

She sent Charles around to all the houses in the neighborhood with a batch of circulars advertising the school. Charles was hopeful; perhaps he too could be a student at the school; perhaps he was going to be educated after all! But no one applied. Charles went back to the pawnbrokers with anything that they could scrape up.

It was the custom in those days for debtors who could not pay their debts to be sent to prison. There were already protests against this law, which was no help to anyone since the debtor, once imprisoned, could not work to pay off his debts, but it was years before the protests had any effect. John Dickens, sued by his creditors, was carried off to the Marshalsea, the big debtor's prison which stood south of the River Thames near to Southwark Cathedral. "The sun," he remarked to the

The house where Charles Dickens lived as a boy

weeping Charles, "has set on me for ever." Later Charles wrote an account of his first visit to his father in prison.

> My father was waiting for me in the lodge and we went up to his room and cried very much. And he told me, I remember, to take warning by the Marshalsea and to observe that if a man had twenty pounds a year, and spent nineteen pounds, nineteen shillings and six pence he would be happy; but that a shilling spent the other way would make him wretched.

John Dickens was not a man to remain gloomy for long. Soon he was sending out for his dinner and dispatching Charles to another prisoner's room to borrow a knife and fork. Charles remembered that there was "something attractive and gypsy-like about the meal."

All these hard early experiences were to furnish Charles Dickens with material for his novels. Mr. and Mrs. Micawber, two of his most famous characters in *David Copperfield*, were caricatures based on certain aspects of his father and mother. The debtor's prison appears in *Pickwick Papers* and in *David Copperfield*; in *Little Dorrit* a large part of the story takes place within the walls of the Marshalsea.

The Navy Board continued to pay his salary to John Dickens while he was in the Marshalsea, but since prisoners there had to buy their own food, coals and candles, there was not enough left for Mrs. Dickens and the young family in Bayham Street. They had nothing more to pawn except absolute necessities.

In this crisis a cousin, James Lamont, turned up with

an offer of help. Charles was now not quite twelve years old, and could begin to earn his living. Lamont offered to get him a job in Warner's Blacking Warehouse, where boys were employed to stick labels on the jars of blacking. Charles would be able to earn six, perhaps later on seven shillings a week.

Mrs. Dickens jumped at the offer and John Dickens agreed. Charles had no choice. He was miserable and furious because he felt bitterly that his parents did not care in the least that he would have no further education. He had secret dreams of a grammar school and a university, but these must now be abandoned. Soon after his twelfth birthday he started work in Warren's Blacking Warehouse at Hungerford Stairs, near the Charing Cross Bridge over the Thames.

3

CHARLES was so miserable in the Blacking Warehouse he could not bring himself even to speak of that time for years to come. When he was a happy and successful novelist in his thirties, he tried to write his autobiography, and was obliged, luckily for all of us, to change it into the novel *David Copperfield* before he could bear to publish the story of those months. He was, as he described the young David, "sunk in a deep sense of abandonment."

Charles really was abandoned. Soon after he began work, his mother decided to move with all her other children except Fanny into the Marshalsea, where debtors were allowed to have their families with them. It was much more economical for them all to live rent free in prison where they could be fairly comfortable on John Dickens' salary, which the merciful Navy Board continued to pay him, and which his creditors could not touch.

Fanny was still at the Royal Academy of Music, and Charles, a wage earner, was not allowed to live in the Marshalsea, though he and Fanny went to dinner there on Sundays. Mrs. Dickens found a room for Charles in a lodging house in Camden, and he started life on his own in London at the age of twelve.

"The blacking warehouse," he wrote in *David Copperfield*, "was the last house at the bottom of a narrow street running down to the river. It was a crazy old house abutting on the water when the tide was in, and on the mud when the tide was out, and literally overrun with rats."

Charles' work was to cover the pots of blacking with a piece of oiled paper, tie them around with string, and then clip the paper closely and neatly so that it looked "as smart as a pot of ointment from a chemist's shop." Then he had to stick a printed label on each pot. It was not difficult work but it was monotonous. His parents paid for his lodging, but he had to provide himself with food and anything else he needed out of his six shillings a week.

He bought a penny cottage loaf and pennyworth of milk for his breakfast, and kept another small loaf, and a quarter of a pound of cheese, for his supper at night. He divided what was left of his money into six parts, and wrapped each one up in a piece of paper labeled with the day of the week. In spite of this he often had no money left by Friday. Sometimes the Sunday dinner at the Marshalsea was his only square meal of the week.

Walking to work in the morning made him so hungry

that he could not resist the stale pastries put out for sale at half price in the doorways of the pastry cooks' shops. This meant that all he could afford for dinner was a slice of pudding.

> I remember two pudding shops between which I was divided according to my finances. One was in the court close to St. Martin's Church. The pudding at that shop was made of currants, and was rather a special pudding; but it was dear, two pennyworth not being larger than a pennyworth of more ordinary pudding. This ordinary pudding was a stout pale pudding, heavy and flabby, with great flat raisins stuck in whole at great distances apart. Many a day did I dine off it.

Charles was still small for his age, and since he could not afford to buy clothes and it never occurred to his parents that he would need any new ones, he grew increasingly shabby. One hot night he walked into the bar of a public house, and said magnificently to the landlord, "What is your best, your very best ale a glass?"

The landlord looked down in astonishment at this tattered little creature. "Twopence half penny," he said, was the price of the Genuine Stunning.

Charles, who must at that moment have acted very much like his father, put down two pennies and a halfpenny on the counter. "Then just draw me a glass of the Genuine Stunning, please, with a good head on it," he said.

The landlord called his wife to come and look at his young customer. They asked Charles what his name was

The boy Dickens orders a glass of the very best ale

and where he lived. Charles, with the wariness of a small animal in the undergrowth, invented answers to all these questions. The landlord served him with the ale, and when he had drunk it, the landlord's wife opened the little door of the bar and gave the boy back his two-pence halfpenny. She stooped down to give him a kiss, "half admiring, half compassionate but all womanly and good."

A young genius must have an unconscious sense of something vital in himself which it is the business of his life to foster and cherish. Charles felt that all his promise was being stifled since he learned nothing at all in the company of rough ignorant boys.

When he left the warehouse he used to wander about the streets. Later when he wrote in *Oliver Twist* about young boys dragged into the London underworld and carefully trained to be pickpockets and thieves, the vividness of his descriptions was enhanced by a shuddering sense that only good luck had preserved him at twelve years old from the same fate.

"But for the mercy of God I might easily have been, for any care that was taken of me, a little robber, a little vagabond."

Misery and bad food increased the stomach cramps from which Charles had always suffered. One day in the blacking factory he was in such acute pain that he had to stop work and lie on the floor. An older boy called Robert Fagin filled empty blacking bottles with hot water and applied them to the pain, so that by the end of the day Charles could stand shakily on his feet.

The kindly Bob Fagin, certain that Charles was not fit to go home alone, insisted on accompanying him. Charles was going that evening to have supper with his parents in the Marshalsea, but he felt all the disgrace of having a father in prison that John Dickens did not feel for himself. Charles was not going to let Bob Fagin know about this. He tried to get rid of the older boy, but Fagin was determined to see him to the door.

At last Charles pointed to one of a row of terrace houses near the Marshalsea, and told Bob that was his home. Afraid that Fagin would watch him until he went right up to the house, Charles dragged himself up the front steps and knocked on the door. With a touch of impish fancy that had somehow survived the day of racking pain and the long walk, he said to the woman who opened the door, "Does Mr. Robert Fagin live here?" Years later he rather ungratefully used the name of Fagin for the villainous old fence in *Oliver Twist*.

Soon after this Charles begged to be allowed to change his lodging to one nearer the Marshalsea, and found a room in Southwark, close to the prison. His landlord here was a friendly, lame old man with a kindly wife and a lame son. They were all very good to Charles and afterward served as models for the Garlend family in *The Old Curiosity Shop*.

On those evenings when he did not go to the Marshalsea, Charles wandered about the streets, and especially explored the waterside creeks and jetties of the great river. It was a rough, wild and often lawless world that the boy observed with his bright eyes. What he was learning was to be of far more use to him than anything he could have learned at school but of course he did not know this, and suffered all the time from a torturing sense of frustration. This period of his life seemed to him endless, though it actually lasted less than a year.

John Dickens' mother died and left him half her savings. There was enough to pay off all his debts, and so release him from the Marshalsea. He was only half pleased, for life in prison had been much easier than earning a living for his family in the outside world. However he took up the struggle again and went on working for the Navy Board. He found a house for his family in Kentish Town, then an even poorer part of London than Camden. Charles lived at home again but went on working in the blacking factory because nobody seemed to think of anything else for him to do.

On his release from prison John Dickens applied to the Navy Board for a retirement pension. An employee of the Navy Board who had been imprisoned for debt was not entitled to a pension, but in consideration of John Dickens' twenty-year service, and of his six children, the Board allowed him £145 a year.

This was not enough to keep and educate a family. John Dickens surprised everyone by a sudden spurt of energy. He learned shorthand, and applied for work as a reporter to his wife's brother, John Barrow, who was editor of a newspaper called *The Mirror of Parliament*.

One day John Dickens happened to pass the warehouse and saw Charles in the window sticking labels on the bottles. John suddenly revolted. This was not suitable work for *his* eldest son. There was no future in this! Charles must leave at once and go to school again.

Elizabeth Dickens objected. Charles' wage, now 7/_ a week, was a great help toward feeding the family. But John, touched in his pride and in his affection, was not to be moved. It was years before Charles forgave his mother for her willingness to sacrifice his chance for an education.

He left the Blacking Warehouse with overwhelming relief, a keen sense of the importance of making a success in life, and a steely determination to achieve it.

◄ 4 ►

CHARLES went to the Wellington Academy in Hampstead Road, where he spent two and a half happy years. When Charles was fifteen his education was supposed to be completed. Somebody once asked John Dickens where his eldest son had been educated. He laughed and replied, "Why, Sir, he may be said to have educated himself."

Charles left school at Eastertime in the year 1827, and found a job as an office boy to a firm of Solicitors, Molloys of Symonds Inn. The new office boy only stayed there six weeks, but it was long enough for him to make a life-long friend, Thomas Mitton, who was a clerk in the same office.

John Dickens, now a successful reporter, solvent for the time being and pleased with himself, thought the job at Molloys not good enough for Charles. In May he secured for him a clerkship in the firm of Ellis and Blackmore who had offices in Gray's Inn. Charles was at first paid 13/6d, but later rose to 15/– a week.

He found his work dull; it consisted mostly of copying letters and documents. He always remembered later how dusty the chambers of Ellis and Blackmore were. "I could take off the distinct impress of my figure on any article of furniture by merely lounging upon it for a few minutes; it used to be a private amusement of mine to print myself off, if I may use the expression, all over the room. It was the first large circulation I had."

But all the time he was watching and listening, storing up impressions of the people who came to the office. In the evenings he went to the theater, always a passion of his, with the other young clerks. When they could not afford tickets they strolled about London watching the people. Seven Dials was one of their favorite haunts. Charles remarked that those who passed through the Dials on a hot summer evening and saw the women of the houses gossiping on their doorsteps would think they were a peaceful community. But,

> The man in the shop ill treats his family; the carpet beater extends his professional pursuits to his wife; the au pair front has an undying feud with the two pair front in consequence of his (the two pair front) persisting in dancing over his (the one pair front's) head; when he and his family have retired for the night, the two pair back *will* interfere with the front kitchen's children; the Irishman comes down drunk every night, and attacks everybody; and the two pair back screams at everything.

When he was not going to the theater or watching the dramas in the streets, Charles read strenuously in the British Museum Library, trying to fill in the gaps in his education. His ambition was turning more and more toward the theater. He went as often as he could afford to the best plays; he studied parts so as to train himself to learn by heart. He even took some lessons in acting, and practiced before a mirror, watching himself enter a room, sit down on a chair, or make a bow.

After some months of this preparation he applied for an audition to the manager of the Covent Garden Theatre, where in those days they performed plays and musical comedies, not just opera and ballet as they do today. The manager gave him an appointment but when the day came a bad cold and a swollen face prevented Charles from going to the theater. Surprisingly he never tried again for an appointment, perhaps because he knew instinctively that he was moving toward another goal.

Meanwhile he was interested in his father's work as a reporter, and he too began to learn shorthand. To get some practice he applied for work as a reporter in the Doctors' Commons. This was a collection of law courts in a quiet backwater to the south of St. Paul's, and in the Doctors' Commons, as Dickens wrote later in *David Copperfield*, "they administer ecclesiastical law, and play all kinds of tricks with obsolete old monsters of Acts of Parliament. It is a place that has a monopoly in suits about peoples' wills, and peoples' marriages, and disputes about ships and boats." Doctors' Commons was abolished in 1857.

Dickens, a satirical and impatient youngster who had no respect for institutions as such, and hated anything slow-moving, came out of the Doctors' Commons with a very unfavorable impression of the law. "I have that high opinion of the law of England generally which one is likely to derive from the impression that it puts all honest men under the diabolical hoofs of all scoundrels."

The time was now coming when something more than his natural impatience made it urgent for him to press on with earning a better living. He fell deeply in love with Maria Beadnell, the daughter of a prosperous banker who lived in Lombard Street, the famous street of Banking Houses. Charles Dickens later drew a portrait of Maria as Dora in *David Copperfield*. She was enchantingly pretty and gay and played the harp. "She was more than human to me. She was a Fairy, a Sylph, I don't know what she was, anything that no one ever saw and everything that everybody ever wanted. I was swallowed up in an abyss of love on the instant."

Maria was not swallowed up in the abyss of love. She liked Charles, he was such a good-looking boy, he had such bright eyes, such a fair complexion; he enlivened any room by coming into it. But he was only seventeen when they met. He was a clerk earning fifteen shillings a week, and Maria, who was a year or two older than he was, knew perfectly well that her father would not consider such a suitor. So she played with Charles, sometimes encouraging him, so that his spirits soared, and sometimes plunging him into despair by withdrawing from him. He could not understand why her feelings for him seemed to change so often, his feelings for her never changed. "She pervaded every chink and crevice of my mind for three or four years." All his life he never forgot the way her hands moved on the harp, the way her eyebrows drew together. The color of a pair of gloves that she once asked him to match for her could send a thrill of shock through his blood to the end of his life.

Climbing up the ladder of the law was much too slow for him. He worked at his shorthand late into the night, though he found it, as David Copperfield was to find it, "about equal in difficulty to the mastery of six languages. The changes that were rung on dots, the wonderful vagaries that were played by circles; the unaccountable consequence that resulted from marks like flies' legs; the tremendous effects of a curve in the wrong place not only troubled my waking hours, but reappeared before me in my sleep."

But, always determined, he now had the hope of Maria Beadnell before him. He made himself into a first-rate shorthand writer, and began to look for work on a newspaper.

In March 1832, soon after his twentieth birthday, he joined the reporting staff on a new paper, the *True Sun*. He was to be a Parliamentary reporter; the first piece of work he did for the *True Sun* was to take down the final speeches made by the Committee discussing the Reform Bill, which when passed was to extend the franchise to a far greater number of people, and in the end to change the character of the British Parliament.

CHARLES Dickens worked as a political reporter in the Gallery of the House of Commons for four years. It was a time of great parliamentary activity. During those years the Reform Bill became law; slavery was abolished in the British colonies; the Corn Laws, which kept up the price of bread by forbidding the importation of corn, were repealed; the Poor Law Bill was introduced to control parish relief for the destitute.

Dickens soon proved himself a first-rate reporter, but he never became closely involved with either political party, Whig or Tory. His sympathies were always with the oppressed. They were also always with the individual against any unnecessary interference by authority. His natural bent was to support anybody who wanted to live in his own way and enjoy himself against anyone who tried to prevent him.

As he sat in the Gallery night after night hearing and

writing down the endless speeches he came to feel no more respect for politics than he had felt for the law. Anything pompous or long-winded bored him. Afterward he often spoke of "the great dust heap of Westminster."

He worked for the *True Sun* for eight months and then resigned to work for the *Mirror of Parliament*, which was edited by his uncle John Henry Barrow. The object of this paper was to produce a word-for-word report of all speeches made in the House of Commons. Charles Dickens was one of the most accurate reporters in the Press Gallery. On one occasion the Chief Secretary, Mr. Stanley, made a very long speech about the Bill for the Suppression of the Disturbances in Ireland. It was the custom for the *Mirror of Parliament* reporters to work in shifts of three quarters of an hour each on a long debate since the Editor thought this was as much as anyone could do at a time with absolute accuracy. Charles reported the first part of Stanley's speech, and then came on again for the last section, another journalist reporting the middle.

When the speech appeared in the *Mirror of Parliament*, the Chief Secretary found the beginning and the end perfectly correct but the middle full of mistakes. He asked Barrow to send around the reporter who had recorded the beginning and the end to take down the whole speech for him so that it could be published correctly in the Irish papers.

When Mr. Stanley walked into the room where Charles Dickens was waiting for him, and saw a slight, pink-cheeked young man of twenty, he frowned and said, "I think there is some mistake. I had hoped to see the gentleman who reported part of my speech." Dickens, blushing ingenuously, replied, "I am that gentleman." When the Chief Secretary had dictated the speech to him and read the script, he sent a note to the editor of the *Mirror of Parliament* thanking him for sending such an excellent stenographer.

As a result Charles got a better job on the *Morning Chronicle*, which was then regarded as the rival of *The Times*. The brilliant young reporter kept a sardonic eye on what he was reporting. When afterward Members of Parliament appeared in his novels they were nearly all subjects for mockery. During the Parliamentary recesses Charles was sent into the country to report local elections. This gave him a wide experience of English life in the provinces as well as in London.

In his private life things were not going so well. Maria Beadnell was still flirting with him in a half-hearted way. She had no real love to give him and when she was with her friends she made fun of his ardent devotion. Charles came to know of this, and began to feel that the relationship was hopeless. He made one last appeal to Maria. "All that anyone can do to raise himself by his own exertions I have done and will do. I never have loved, I never shall love any human creature breathing but yourself."

Maria shrank away from the intensity of his feeling, and answered him coldly. He still loved her. "When we were falling off one another," he wrote later, "I came from the House of Commons many a night at two to three o'clock in the morning only to wander past the place she was asleep in." But he saw that it was no good, and he was not prepared to be played with any longer. He returned her letters and presents and said goodbye.

There were other troubles. John Dickens was arrested for debt again on the suit of a firm of wine merchants. Charles could not pay off the debt because he had to use all the money he could raise to support his mother and the younger children. He told a friend that his salary was completely mortgaged for weeks to come, but added, "I am determined to see everything in as bright a light as possible." It was the first of the family burdens that he was to take on his shoulders with great generosity and cheerfulness for the rest of his life.

Meanwhile he was moving almost casually toward his vocation. He was growing tired of taking down other men's words. He wanted to write something of his own about all the interesting things and the varieties of people he came across. He called what he wrote "Sketches." One day he put a copy of a sketch, *A Dinner in Poplar Walk*, into the mailbox of a periodical called *The Monthly Magazine*.

He heard no more about it. the *Monthly Magazine* cost half a crown, and since Charles was keeping the family he was very hard up, but he managed to spare half a crown, and bought the next issue of the *Monthly Magazine* at Chapman and Hall's shop in the Strand. He opened the magazine in the street and saw his own sketch printed in it. He burst into tears, and could not read a word of the paper which he held in his shaking hand.

He walked into Westminster Hall, and stayed there for a few minutes to compose himself. He dried his eyes and read his sketch. Then still trembling from the shock of happiness he walked on to the House of Commons to begin his evening's reporting. That was in December 1833 when Charles Dickens was twenty-one years old.

6

DICKENS, although only twenty-one, started his career as a published writer with a rich capital of experience to draw upon. Behind him he had memories of a happy childhood but also the knowledge of poverty and family disgrace, of hunger and hardship. His apprenticeship to the law had brought him in contact with many of the odd quirks of human nature. His years in the Press Gallery of the House of Commons had shown him the machinery of government. His journeys as a reporter during the parliamentary recesses had given him a varied knowledge of English provincial life. He had been wholeheartedly in love and had experienced the pain of rejection. He had read widely, if patchily, and his life then as always was enriched by many friendships. It was magnificent equipment for a young novelist, soon to be magnificently used.

He did not at first think of writing novels. He set out to present real people and incidents. He wrote sketches for the *Monthly Magazine*, and soon for the *Morning Chronicle* as well. He wrote under his own name for the *Monthly Magazine*, but for the *Chronicle* adopted the pseudonym of "Boz," which was the family pet name of his youngest brother.

As Boz he soon began to make a name for himself. He attracted the attention of fellow authors, and one of them, the historical novelist William Harrison Ainsworth, invited Dickens to his home. There he met the publisher, John Macrone. Dickens and Macrone walked away from Ainsworth's house together, and the publisher suggested to the young author that he bring out a volume of his sketches. Dickens of course was delighted. He would write more sketches if there were not enough for a volume; he had a lot of notes to work up, and he would go anywhere, see anything that Macrone thought would make a good subject. He had tried his hand at one or two short stories, and if Macrone agreed he would like to include them.

The book was published on Dickens' twenty-fourth birthday, February 7th 1836. Its cumbrous title was: *"Sketches by Boz. Illustrative of Every Day Life and People."*

The sketches were divided into *Scenes* and *Characters*, and there was a separate section called *Our Parish*, which included descriptions of a beadle, that is the officer who administered parish relief, a schoolmaster, a broker's man, the ladies' society, and our next door neighbor. The

Scenes which were not included in *Our Parish*, were all pictures of London life. Among them were descriptions of *Scotland Yard*, the *Law Courts*, *A Pawn Broker's Shop*, *The House of Commons*, *Seven Dials*, the *River*, *Criminal Courts* and *Gin Shops*.

The volume also included a dozen tales which were based on people or incidents that Dickens had observed, but to which he supplied an imaginary explanation or climax. The stories were not as good as the sketches, Dickens the journalist was already expert in handling his material; Dickens the novelist was only just starting. But both sketches and stories showed the first signs of that abundance of life and richness, that keen, satirical humor, and that sympathy with the unprivileged and the unpretentious which were to inform all his work. *Sketches by Boz* are much less read now than any Dickens novel, but when they came out they immediately attracted the attention of reviewers, who saw that a new talent was appearing. Meanwhile life was opening out for Dickens in another direction. He wrote a few sketches for the *Evening Chronicle* whose Editor, George Hogarth, asked the new contributor to his house.

Hogarth had nine children including three pretty daughters, Catherine, Mary and Georgina, who were just growing up. Actually, Catherine—or Kate was already grown-up. Dickens soon became very much at home with the Hogarth girls. They already had plenty of young men around them, but they were delighted with Papa's new contributor, who was so handsome and sparkling, had such bright eyes, and such flowing brown

Titlepage for Charles Dickens' Sketches by Boz
Drawing by George Cruikshank

hair. Above all he was so amusing! He talked so enter-
tainingly and knew so many funny songs!

He was not a bit like the other young men, who
seemed quite stupid and ordinary compared to him. He
had such wonderfully droll ideas that no one else ever
thought of. One day he came to their house dressed as
a sailor, and pranced into the drawing room through the
open French window, dancing a hornpipe, and accompanying himself by whistling. He danced around the
room and then leapt out onto the lawn again; only a
few minutes later he rang the front doorbell, and was
shown in wearing his ordinary clothes and looking intensely serious. The three Miss Hogarths nearly died
laughing.

Dickens was just beginning to recover, though perhaps he never did quite recover, from the soreness left
by Maria Beadnell. There was a great emptiness in his
heart. He missed the pleasure of being loved. He was
young, the Hogarth house was pleasant and welcoming,
all the girls were charming, but Kate was the one old
enough to be married so naturally he fell in love with
Kate. He became engaged to her early in 1835 while
Sketches by Boz were still in the hands of the publishers,
who were waiting for the artist George Cruickshank to
finish the illustrations.

Catherine Hogarth was plump, pretty, and fresh looking, with large, heavy-lidded blue eyes, a small red
mouth, a good forehead and a slightly receding chin. She
had a sweet smile which lit up her face very pleasantly,
but she was indolent and often depressed. She was in-

clined to make a fuss about any small ailment, and to
expect Charles to be as much concerned about a cold or
headache of hers as she was.

When she caught scarlet fever Charles certainly concerned himself; he called constantly to ask after her, and
sent his young brother Fred around with a jar of black
currant jam for her throat, and with some chloride of
lime "to purify the atmosphere of her room." But he
tried to make her understand that he was working under
very great pressure. He could not come to her as often
as she wanted him. When he did not she became petu-
lant and complained that he was making her unhappy
and "cross." Charles wrote to her.

"You will be disappointed—I would rather you would
be—at not seeing me; but you cannot feel vexed at my
doing my best with the stake I have to play for,—you
and a home for both of us." He added rather high-
handedly, "I perceive you have not yet subdued some
part of your disposition—your distrustful feelings and
want of confidence . . . I love you far too well to be
hurt by what in anyone else would have annoyed me
greatly."

These little quarrels were always made up, but they
already indicated a certain lack of true understanding
between the two young people. Life in a prosperous
home had always been easy for Kate Hogarth. Life had
seldom been easy for Charles Dickens and at the moment, when he was carrying on with his work as a
reporter and at the same time making a vigorous start
on his career as a novelist, when he had all his own family

on his shoulders and was living in his room in Furnival's Inn with no dishes, no curtains, no carpets, and with only one shabby blue suit, and a ragged office coat to work in, he could not understand how what seemed trifles to him could be such serious matters to the sheltered girl. He loved her or thought he did, he was longing to get married, but he was also wrapped up in the appearance of his first book. He had no time to ask himself if once again he had given his heart to a young woman who could not fully respond to him.

About a month before the publication of *Sketches by Boz*, Dickens received a new offer. Mr. Hall of the publishing house of Chapman and Hall asked him to write a series of articles on sport. Hall had already engaged the well-known artist, Robert Seymour, to draw a series of illustrations of the adventures of a band of amateur sportsmen who were to be called the Nimrod Club.

Dickens did not welcome the suggestion with any enthusiasm. He thought it would be better for him to write some articles first, and for the illustrations to spring naturally from his text. He said that he was no great sportsman, and would much prefer to write about "a freer range of English scenes and people which I'm afraid I should do in any case whatever course I might prescribe to myself at starting."

Having thus made his position clear he set to work on what was to be the first number of *The Pickwick Papers*.

Seymour had drawn the four characters—Mr. Pickwick "an observer of human nature" with his bald head, his large round spectacles, his kind eyes beaming behind his glasses; Mr. Tupman so stout that he could not see his own watch chain across his stomach, and the folds of his double chin; the poetic Mr. Snodgrass with his large fur-collared blue cloak; Mr. Winkle, in green shooting coat, plaid neck cloth, and close-fitting drab knickers.

Probably because he felt cramped by having to breathe life into another man's characters Dickens found the first number of *The Pickwick Papers* heavy going. Even in this number he began to introduce other characters of his own, beginning with the boastful and talkative Alfred Jingle.

Sketches by Boz were selling vigorously. The first issue of *The Pickwick Papers* was due to appear on March 1st. Charles decided that he was in a position to get married. He did not want to wait while the bans were read. He was never fond of waiting, so he applied for a special licence, and married Catherine Hogarth on April 2, 1836 in St. Luke's Church, Chelsea.

They spent a week's honeymoon in the country near Rochester which was always connected in Charles' mind with the happiest years of his childhood.

He was so unaccustomed to vacations that he was restless, and he began to realize now that he was alone with her that Kate was not the most stimulating companion, though she was gentle and affectionate. He tried to turn one of his sketches into a play to amuse her, worked when he could get time to himself on the next issue of *Pickwick Papers*, and was glad at the end of the week to go back to Furnival's Inn where the young couple

Mrs. Charles Dickens

were going to live in rooms which Charles already occupied.

Trouble began at once about the illustrations that Seymour had prepared for the second issue of *Pickwick*. Dickens wanted them altered to suit what he was writing. Seymour, twelve years older than Dickens, was an established artist with a high reputation. He was also quarrelsome, vain, and very nervous. Dickens had sincere respect for him, but was determined to have his own way with a book that was rapidly developing in his mind. He asked, courteously but firmly, for some alterations in the drawings. Seymour agreed to make them, went home, and started work on them, then suddenly threw down his pencil, rushed out into the garden and shot himself.

Chapman and Hall had based their idea for the book on Seymour's drawings, and their hope of selling it mostly on Seymour's reputation. They wanted to drop the whole thing, but Dickens was now firmly committed to Pickwick, and persuaded them to look for another artist.

Among other young men who applied for the work was the future great novelist William Makepeace Thackeray. Chapman and Hall, guided by Dickens, finally chose another young artist called Hablôt K. Browne, who signed his drawings with the pseudonym of "Phiz." Phiz proved to be a splendid interpreter for Boz and illustrated his books for the next twenty years.

Chapman and Hall must have had several uneasy moments, for the first four issues of *Pickwick Papers* did not sell, and it looked as though from their point of view the whole expensive venture might be a failure. But Dickens the novelist was finding himself. In the fifth number he introduced the first of his glorious comic characters, Sam Weller, whom Mr. Pickwick discovered cleaning boots in the yard of a London Inn. "He was habited in a coarse striped waistcoat, with black calico sleeves, and blue glass buttons; drab breeches and leggings. A bright red handkerchief was wound in a very loose and unstudied style around his neck, and an odd little hat was carelessly thrown on the side of his head.

"Sam," the chambermaid called out. "No 22 wants his boots."

"Ask No. 22 whether he'll have 'em now or wait until he gets them. Who's Number 22 to put all the others out? No, no, regular rotation as Jack Ketch (the hangman) said when he tied men up."

The bustling old landlady of the White Hart made her appearance in the opposite gallery.

"Sam! Where's that lazy, idle . . . why don't you answer?"

"Wouldn't be genteel to answer till you done talking, Mam."

Sam, a Cockney humorist, a philosopher, always good-natured, shrewd, observant, lively, with unlimited nerve, delighted the readers of *Pickwick Papers* from the first. Mr. Pickwick engaged him as his personal servant, so that Sam took part in every adventure of the four sportsmen, and enlivened every scene with his racy comments.

Mrs. Bardell Faints in Mr. Pickwick's Arms
From Pickwick Papers

The Pickwick Papers are a rambling chronicle rather than a story. Dickens was still half a reporter; he used his four characters, and the attendant Sam as observers, taking them to an election, a cricket match, a Christmas house party in the country; into the law courts where the innocent Mr. Pickwick surprisingly finds himself sued by his landlady for breach of a promise to marry her which he never even thought of making, and into the debtors' prisons where Pickwick goes because he will not pay the damages with which the court of law unjustly charged him.

Mr. Pickwick moves through all these scenes, guileless, kind, observing everything with an eager interest. He has the qualities of simplicity, gentleness, and unpretentiousness which Dickens loved. Sam follows him, using his shrewd knowledge of the world to keep his master out of trouble when he can, and with as little reverence for blown-up authority as Dickens himself had.

> "Where do you live?" the magistrate said to Sam.
> "Vare ever I can," replied Sam.
> "Put that down Mr. Jinks," said the magistrate who was fast rising into a rage.
> "Score it under," said Sam.
> "He is a vagabond, Mr. Jinks," said the magistrate, "he is a vagabond on his own statement. Is he not, Mr. Jinks? I'll commit him. I'll commit him as such."
> "This is a very impartial country for justice," said Sam. "There ain't a magistrate going as don't commit himself twice as often as he commits other people."

Other amusing characters drift across the pages of this haphazard chronicle, which has all Dickens' richness and abounding life. There is Old Mr. Weller, Sam's father, the stagecoach driver, who puts up as good naturedly as he can with the lectures of his shrewish second wife; the snobbish Mrs. Leo Hunter who spends her time trying to persuade famous people to come to her house, and is very easily duped into thinking anybody famous; the two lively medical students, Bob Sawyer, and Benjamen Allen whose parties at their lodgings are overshadowed by fear of the landlady whose bill they haven't paid. All these and many more fill up the crowded pages so that the reader does not so much remember that he is reading a book as feel that he is moving about in a world.

Once Sam Weller had appeared in the book and Dickens felt able to let his invention play freely with other characters *The Pickwick Papers* began to have a great success. On July 25th Dickens wrote to his other publisher Macrone, *"Pickwick Triumphant."* Chapman and Hall raised his payment for the monthly installments. He had hopes of writing a play, and he was being pressed to write a children's book. He decided that the moment had come to give up his regular work as a reporter in the Gallery of the House of Commons, and to live and keep his wife and the child they were now expecting by his original writing alone.

AFTER a holiday in the country, during which Dickens tried to write a farce for the stage, he and Kate came back to Furnival's Inn, he to earn his living by writing, she to make baby clothes. Charles, who was becoming well-known, was out and about a great deal when he was not writing. Kate needed company: her sister Mary came in the Fall to stay with them.

Mary was sixteen, pretty, gay, graceful, intelligent. She adored her gifted brother-in-law, and was intensely interested in his work. Both he and Kate were very fond of her, and since Kate, who was never energetic, was now unwilling to go out much, Mary went everywhere with Charles. He enjoyed her company, and basked in her appreciation. It was a very happy time in his life, for the world was opening out to him on all sides.

He was asked by the publisher, Richard Bentley, to edit a magazine and to write a serial for it. *Pickwick* was going splendidly. Dickens was asked to many houses where he had never been before, and was meeting the famous editors and writers of his day.

Leigh Hunt, an editor of great experience, and friend of Keats, Shelley and Byron, wrote of Charles Dickens:

> What a face it is to meet in a drawing room! It has the life and soul of fifty human beings in it.

Thomas Carlyle wrote a description of Charles Dickens:

> He is a fine little fellow, Boz, I think: clear, blue intelligent eyes that he arches amazingly; large, protrusive rather loose mouth; a face of the most extreme mobility, which he shuttles about, eyebrows, eyes, mouth and all . . . in a very singular manner while speaking. Surmount this with a loose coil of common-coloured hair, set it on a small compact figure, very small, dressed a la D'r Orsay (that is, like a dandy) rather than well. For the rest a quiet, shrewd-looking little fellow, who seems to guess pretty well what he is and what others are.

This description was said by other observers to be inaccurate. Dickens' eyes were hazel rather than blue, his height was five feet eight inches; he was not very small, though no doubt he seemed so to the tall Carlyle. Dickens' hair was described by most of those who knew him as a rich brown. But everyone seems to have agreed on the brilliance of his eyes, and the constant movement of his face, which showed his every feeling.

Dickens loved jewelry, fancy waistcoats, and elaborately cut coats. His complexion was so fair that he looked younger than he was, but the impression he made on people was one of energy and decision.

"He was spirited in his manner and bearing; he struck everybody as having a great deal of practical sense," wrote Carlyle's wife, Jane. She added, "His features often looked as if they were made of steel."

Dickens now began to write a serial for the Bentley magazine which he called *Oliver Twist*.

The Dickens baby, a boy, was born in January 1837, and was named Charles. There was no longer room for the family in the Furnival's Inn chambers, especially since Mary Hogarth was still living with them. She and Charles went househunting, and found what they wanted at 48 Doughty Street, which is now the headquarters of the Dickens Fellowship. They moved there in April. Dickens, with his wife and his first child, his charming young sister-in-law, his engrossing work and his new house, was on top of the world.

Then came a tragic blow. On the evening of May 6th Dickens took Kate and Mary to the theater. When they came home at one o'clock, Mary went up to bed "in perfect health and in her usual delightful spirits." She was taken ill while she was undressing. A doctor was called, but her heart had collapsed, and she died in Charles' arms.

His grief was overwhelming. Without realizing it he had found Mary better company than Kate. He wrote her epitaph. "Young, beautiful, and good, God in his mercy numbered her among his angels at the early age

Charles Dickens, his wife and her sister

of seventeen." Dickens never forgot her, and the portrait of a lovely, gentle and affectionate young girl, half woman, half child, who appears in several of his novels, is his real memorial to Mary Hogarth.

Charles was unable to write for a time; both *Pickwick* and *Oliver Twist* were held up. He and Kate went abroad for a vacation in Belgium. In spite of his deep grief Dickens was stimulated by his first crossing of the Channel into Europe, and was eager to go again when he could hope to be in better spirits to enjoy it. He came back to Doughty Street, and at once resumed work on the two books.

Oliver is born in a workhouse, to which his mother, picked up on the road in a state of exhaustion, has been carried. She wears no wedding ring and there is no evidence of her past except a locket with some initials on it, which is stolen from her neck by the nurse who is supposed to be looking after her. She dies an hour after her son is born. Oliver Twist, given his names by Mr. Bumble, the Beadle, is brought up by the parish.

Mr. Bumble has, as was customary in those days, a great deal of power. He is a mean-spirited bully and the children under his care are miserable and half-starved. Oliver gets into deep disgrace one day at dinner time by asking for more. "Asking for more like Oliver Twist" has become a usual phrase. Indeed *Oliver Twist* is one of the most widely known of Dickens' novels.

Oliver, after being apprenticed to a local undertaker whose wife bullies him, runs away to London, where he falls into the hands of a villainous old Jew, Fagin. Fagin

Illustration by George Cruikshank for Oliver Twist

runs a thieves' kitchen in which he receives stolen goods and trains young boys as pickpockets. Among his followers and allies are a cocky and expert boy thief known as The Artful Dodger; a brutal burglar named Bill Sykes; and Nancy, the girl who loves Bill Sykes and works with him, but who has enough human feeling left to pity and try to protect Oliver who is, she sees, too honest as well as too gentle, and delicate for such a life.

The book is the story of Oliver's rescue by good people; of his recapture by the thieves, and of his final escape in circumstances that lead to the discovery of his parentage.

The vivid descriptions of Fagin's headquarters are pervaded by the sense of horror which Dickens always felt about that underworld of London, which he had glimpsed as a child living alone in the great city. Oliver's experiences are those which might easily have fallen to the lot of the small boy who wandered the streets at night after his day's work in the blacking warehouse. Dickens had a tremendous gift for evoking physical surroundings. As we read *Oliver Twist* we almost feel and smell the dirt and squalor of the Thieves' Kitchen, which is the expression of their moral degradation. The relief of Oliver's escape is like waking up from a nightmare.

As *Oliver Twist* appeared in monthly numbers there was a loud outcry against it in some quarters. Those who supported the Poor Law of the time were particularly angry because Dickens has shown so clearly what could happen to an orphan child if parish relief were administered by a beadle with as little humanity as Mr. Bumble. Other critics thought the book too squalid; they did not like to be obliged to face what was going on in the underworld of their own city. But Dickens' fellow authors, especially the novelist Anthony Trollope, admired *Oliver Twist* enormously, and Boz had a growing number of faithful readers.

8

Iт was while he was writing *Pickwick* and *Oliver Twist*
that Dickens first met John Forster, who was to play an
important part in his life, and to write the first full-length
biography of him after his death.

Forster, a man of the same age as Dickens, was born
at Newcastle-on-Tyne. He was the son of a cattle dealer.
An uncle paid for his education, first at a private school,
then at University College, London. He became a law
student at the Inner Temple in London.

Forster was an active, able, ambitious young man determined to rise in the world and not only in the world
of law. He was interested in writers and writing. In the
year 1832, when he was only twenty, he managed to get
himself appointed drama critic on the *True Sun*. Soon
he was writing criticisms of books as well as of plays for
three newspapers, and at the age of twenty-two he became the chief literary and drama critic on the *Examiner*,

a leading periodical of the day. Forster continued to write for all the best literary journals. He also wrote biographies of Oliver Goldsmith and of Walter Savage Landor.

He did not entirely neglect the law. He managed by besieging the Chancellor, Lord Bingham, to secure an appointment as a Commissioner for Lunacy. This was a nominal position which involved very little work but carried a salary of £1500 a year. It was just what John Forster wanted. It provided him with a basic living and left him plenty of time for writing and for what he liked nearly as much, getting to know interesting people and taking a hand in their affairs.

John Forster was short and stocky with a big head, strong features, and a pugnacious jaw. He always wore a short frock coat, tightly buttoned up, and made great play with a single eyeglass. He assumed an air of authority that made him seem much older than he was. He could be a most valuable friend.

"When anybody is in trouble," Thackeray wrote, "we all fly to him for refuge, he is omniscient, and works miracles." In fact he did for various authors at different times what a good literary agent does today. He supervised their contracts, advised them on terms with their publishers and smoothed out practical difficulties.

John Forster could on the other hand be possessive, overbearing and quarrelsome. He took on the young Robert Browning, and trumpeted praise of his work all over London, but he soon irritated the poet so much that only swift action by another guest at a dinner party prevented Browning from throwing a decanter at Forster's head.

Forster now met Charles Dickens, and very soon took over the management of his affairs.

It was about time for somebody to manage them. Dickens had involved himself in an awful mess. He was still writing both *Pickwick Papers* and *Oliver Twist* for serial publication. He was editing the *Bentley Miscellany*. He had promised Macrone, who had published *Sketches by Boz*, an entirely new novel which he planned to call *Gabriel Varden, the Locksmith of London*. He had promised a children's book to somebody else, and two more novels that he had not even thought of to Bentley. All this was partly because now that he had given up reporting he was anxious to accept every commission from a publisher to ensure earning a living for himself and his family. But he was suddenly overcome when he realized that he had taken on far more than he could hope to carry out.

"Why even Sir Walter Scott himself could not have coped with all these," Dickens exclaimed despairingly as he poured out the story to Forster. Forster promised help and at once took over all Dickens' proofreading so as to give him more time for his writing.

Part of the trouble was that since all Dickens' agreements with his publishers had been made before his swift rise to fame, his own percentage of the profits on his books was much lower than he now had a right to expect. To add to the confusion, Macrone was proposing to reprint *Sketches by Boz* in the same green covers in which Chapman and Hall were bringing out *Pickwick Papers*. John Forster now took all this in hand and made excellent arrangements with Chapman and Hall, who bought up the book rights of *Sketches by Boz*, and of *Oliver Twist*, which was still appearing in Bentley's Magazine. Since Chapman and Hall owned the rights to *The Pickwick Papers*, this now enabled them to publish all three of them in the same book form. Forster made good terms with them, and they remained Dickens' publishers for the next six years.

Forster, in spite of occasional quarrels, in spite of the fact that his managing ways often irritated Dickens, remained his friend and business manager for life. Forster was a trying guest at a dinner party; he shouted everybody else down and could not bear to be contradicted. Alone with one friend, he was sympathetic, helpful and kind. It was to him that Dickens first talked or wrote when he had a new idea for a book. It was Forster's company, especially in these early years, that he wanted most often.

There was a strong contradiction in the nature of Charles Dickens. He was a born writer and loved writing, but he hated sitting still. Nor was he satisfied with a quiet domestic life. After a long day's work he would scribble a note and send it by express to Forster's house.

"I intend ordering an 'oss to be at this door in the morning to convey me a fifteen mile ride out, ditto in, and a lunch on the road. Can you spare time to join me? We will return here to dinner at 5."

Another note said, "I think Richmond and Twickenham through the Park, out at Knightsbridge and through Barnes Common would make a beautiful ride. I sent Fred down now in agonies of despair to know if you were going."

Again, "Muffle yourself up and start off with me for a good brisk walk over Hampstead Heath. I know a good 'ous," (this was the Inn at the top of the Heath called Jack Straw's Castle) "where we can have a red hot chop for dinner and a bottle of good wine."

"My missis is going out to dinner," he wrote another time, "Do come here and sit here and read or work or do something while I write . . . which will be after a lamb chop."

There were other exciting friends whose company was always a relief after the long hours spent alone at work. One evening at Covent Garden, Forster introduced Dickens to the actor, William Charles Macready, who although nearly twenty years older than Dickens, became a boon companion. Dickens was still very friendly with Harrison Ainsworth, at whose house he had met his first publisher. There he also met a young Irish artist, Daniel Maclise, who became one of his greatest friends. Thomas Mitton, the lawyer, was still a staunch friend with whom Dickens had never lost touch since his first job as an office boy. There was the novelist, William Thackeray, who had applied for the job of illustrating *Pickwick Papers* and had failed to get it, and the young illustrator Hablôt Browne who had gotten it. Dickens was happy in the company of all or any of these, and ready to go on a vacation with any of them at times that did not interfere with his writing.

He had another great friend, a woman who for a long time played an important part in his life. She was Angela Georgina Burdett-Coutts, a very rich young woman whose sole ambition was to use her money as far as possible to relieve the distress of the poor, especially in London where she lived. She spent all her energies and the better part of her fortune fighting against bad drainage, bad housing, and the lack of food, warmth, clothing, and education which caused so much misery.

Angela first met Dickens when he was a young reporter, and she was twenty-one and had just come into the management of her own fortune. She found in Dickens someone who knew a great deal about the bad conditions of life in London and whose sympathies for the poor were keen and knowledgeable.

They began to work together. He advised her on the best way to use her money to relieve these hardships; the things they came across increased Dickens' knowledge of that dark underworld of which he had already, as a little boy, had frightening glimpses, and of which he had again seen something from the law courts and as a reporter.

His friendship with Angela Burdett-Coutts lasted for many years, and as his own earnings increased with his success he too helped with money as well as with advice. This serious friendship and the unceasing social work that was the substance of it was a quiet strand in Dickens' life altogether apart from his more boisterous relationships with his men friends. He was never in love with Angela though he valued her highly. If she was in love with him, and it seemed probable that she did love him deeply, she kept it out of sight. It is possible that she may have been in Dickens' mind when later on he drew the character of Agnes Wickfield in *David Copperfield*.

In the meantime, for all his pleasure in these growing friendships, for all the new demands of married life, Dickens was writing furiously. His invention was so rich that an idea for his next novel often came to him while he was finishing the current book. He had barely written the last words of the last installment of *Oliver Twist* before he was writing the first words of *Nicholas Nickleby*.

9

At that time there were a number of bad boarding schools in England, most of which happened to be situated in Yorkshire: probably because it was a long way from London, and the owners hoped to escape notice. Unwanted stepchildren, illegitimate children, and orphans with indifferent guardians were sent to these schools.

Dickens had heard about them in his childhood; he knew a boy in Chatham who came home with a poisoned abscess because the headmaster hadn't bothered to get a doctor, but had lanced it himself with a dirty penknife. Now somebody, probably Angela Burdett-Coutts, reminded him that these schools still existed. Dickens' imagination and his compassionate indignation were both fired. He went off to Yorkshire to see for himself, taking with him Hablôt Browne, who, as "Phiz," had illustrated *Sketches by Boz*. They presented themselves to the headmaster of a school at Bowes as friends of a widow who wanted to find a school for her boys.

The headmaster suspected them of snooping and turned them away after five minutes. Five minutes were enough for Dickens to gather the material he wanted. The school at Bowes became Dotheboys Hall to which the young Nicholas Nickleby went as assistant master. The headmaster paid dearly for his summary dismissal of his visitors; he was immortalized as Wackford Squeers, at once a gloriously comic character and an exposure of his kind, although Dickens was careful to state: "Mr. Squeers is the representative of a class, not of an individual. Mr. Squeers and his school are a faint and feeble picture of an existing reality."

Dotheboys Hall provided only one episode in the novel of *Nicholas Nickleby*. At that time the general idea of a novel was still a story with a hero and a heroine, who after difficulties and adventures came together in the end and were married. Dickens so far had not followed this pattern. The central figure in *Pickwick Papers* was an elderly man; the central figure in *Oliver Twist* was a boy. Nicholas was his first real hero, a young man setting out to make his fortune in the world and to support his widowed mother and his sister. It is true that the heroine of *Nicholas Nickleby*, Madeleine Bray, only appears halfway through the book, and is not much more than a cardboard figure when she does appear. The real heroine is Kate, Nicholas' sister, who is a slightly more real character than Madeleine. She is a modern character in one way, for she sets out as Nicholas does to try and earn her living in a hard world, and she does this not by being a governess, which was almost the only occupation considered suitable in life or fiction for gently nurtured young women of the time.

Nicholas Nickleby has not only a hero and heroine but a villain, Ralph Nickleby, almost as wicked an uncle as the one who planned the murder of the Babes in the Wood. It is he who introduces the innocent Kate, meaning her for a decoy, to the vague philanderer Lord Frederick Verisopht, and his friend the seducer, Sir Mulbery Hawk, who dogs her footsteps until she is once again under her brother's protection.

While she is struggling in London, Nicholas, who has arrived full of vigor and hope at his first post in the Yorkshire School, is listening with growing astonishment to Mr. Squeers' method of taking a class in "English Spelling and Philosophy."

"Now then," the headmaster said, "Where's the first boy?"

"Please sir, he's cleaning the back parlor window."

"So he is to be sure," rejoined Squeers. "We go on the practical method of teaching, Nickleby. c.l.e.a.n. verb, active, to make bright, to scour, w.i.n.d.e.r. winder, a casement. When the boy knows this out of a book he goes and does it. It's just the same principle as the use of globes. Where's the second boy?"

"Please, Sir, he's weeding the garden," replied a small voice.

"To be sure," said Squeers by no means disconcerted, "So he is. b.o.t. bot, t.i.n. tin, n.e.y. Bottinney, noun substantive, a knowledge of plants. When he has learned that bottinney is a knowledge of plants he goes and knows them. That's our system, Nickleby."

Although Nicholas makes a good friend in the neighborhood in the genial Yorkshireman, John Browdie, it is clear that he will not be able to stand Dotheboys Hall for long, and he is soon on his travels again, taking with him Smike, the poor half-starved drudge of the school who has been unmercifully bullied by both Mr. and Mrs. Squeers.

Nicholas' next adventure is with a traveling theatrical company, owned by an old actor manager Vincent Crummles. The Crummles move from one town to another heroically performing plays with such fragments of scenery and props as they have been able to get together, and with a tendency to give all the best parts to themselves and their growing family, of whom one, a skinny little girl generally dressed in a green gauze bonnet trimmed with a pink rose, is known as *The Infant Phenomenon*. She sings and dances and plays excruciatingly badly all the juvenile parts. Her talent is inherited, for Mrs. Crummles, mother of six, is never at a loss on the stage.

"I pledge you my professional word," said Mr. Crummles shaking his head gravely. "I didn't know she *could* dance until her last benefit, and then she played Juliet and Helen Macgreggor, and did the skipping rope hornpipe between the pieces. The very first time I saw that admirable woman," said Mr. Crummles in a tone of

Mr. Linkinwater intimates his approval of Nicholas

confidential friendship. "She stood upon her head on the butt-end of a spear surrounded by blazing fireworks."

While Nicholas is rewriting old plays to suit these enchanting people, and acting any parts in them which they don't want themselves, Kate is having her own richly comic adventures in London. She works in the millinery business of Madame Mantalini, who runs it to earn a living for herself and for the idle husband whom she adores. Mr. Mantalini constantly wheedles her out of any attempt to make him work as well. She is so lucky, he points out to her. Two countesses and a dowager have been dying of love for him, and would have been only too glad to marry him and support him.

"Two countesses?" whimpered Madame Mantalini. "You told me one before."

"Two," cried Mantalini, "Two dem'd fine women, real countesses and splendid fortunes, demmit."

"And why didn't you marry them?"

"Why didn't I? Had I not seen at a morning concert, the demndest little fascinator in all the world, and while that little fascinator is my wife may not all the countesses in England be demned."

He coaxes money out of the helpless Madame Mantalini whose business is on the verge of failing.

"You can't want any more just now," she pleads.

"My life and soul," replied her husband. "There is a horse for sale at Scrubbs which it would be a sin and a crime to lose, going, my sense's joy, for nothing."

"For nothing," replied Madame, "I'm glad of that."

"For actually nothing," replied Mantalini. "A hundred guineas down will buy him, mane and crest, legs and tail, and all of the demndest beauty. I will ride him in the Park before the very chariot of the rejected countesses. The demn'd old dowager will faint with grief and rage. The other two will say, He is married, he has made away with himself, it is a demn'd thing, it is all up. They will hate you demnably and wish you dead."

Mr. Mantalini can always coax money out of his unfortunate wife by flattery. Her outline is superb, he tells her, while "The countesses had no outlines at all and the dowager had a demn'd outline."

Meanwhile Mrs. Nickleby, the mother of Nicholas and Kate, keeps up a rambling commentary on things past and present.

"I can't help thinking," mused Mrs. Nickleby, "that she caught cold in that hackney coach going home. Hackney coaches are such nasty things that it is better to walk at any time, for although I believe that a hackney coachman can be transported for life if he has a broken window, still they are so reckless that they nearly all have broken windows. I once had a swelled face for a week from riding in a hackney coach. I think it was a hackney coach," said Mrs. Nickleby reflecting, "though I am not quite certain whether it wasn't a chariot. At all events I know it was dark green with a very long number beginning with a nought and ending with a nine, no beginning with a nine and ending with a nought, that was it, and of course the stamp office people would know at once whether it was a coach or chariot if inquiries were made there. I think it was the very same hackney coach that we found out afterwards had the top open all the time and we should never have known it if they hadn't charged a shilling extra an hour for having it open . . . which is seen was the law then, and a shameful law it appears to be . . . I should say the Corn Laws could be nothing to *that* Act of Parliament."

There are so many passages in *Nicholas Nickleby* which make you feel how very much Dickens must have enjoyed writing them. It was said that Mrs. Nickleby has a distant likeness to his own mother, but Dickens was a writer who could change a pumpkin into a coach and horses. One small habit or mannerism observed in real life, was enough for him to transform it into a whole person.

Nicholas Nickleby is the gayest of his novels. Nicholas and Kate have more adventures and misadventures than there is space to mention here, but they find kind friends. In fact the Cheeryable brothers, who take them under their wing, are almost too kind, sentimentalized in the way that Dickens at his worst could sentimentalize. The novel, sparkling all over with fun and crowded with amusing characters and scenes, comes to a happy ending for both Kate and Nicholas.

There are some books that, mostly because of the author's steadily growing reputation, are successful almost before they are published. Fifty thousand copies of the first monthly number of *Nicholas Nickleby* were sold on the day of publication. There was an immediate attempt to make it into a play without any permission from or payment to the author. Dickens had already suffered from a stage performance of *Oliver Twist* which had been concocted without his permission, and which he disliked so much that he lay down on the floor of his box during the first act and refused to get up again. Stage versions of his books were never at that time good and were a constant irritation, since there were no laws, as there are now, to protect the author's copyright of his work and anybody could seize upon a novel even before it had finished appearing serially and could make a play from it.

Dickens still loved the theater and with his great friend, the actor Macready, started a Shakespeare Club, but it came to an end because John Forster quarreled with most of the other members.

Dickens, whenever he was not working, was extremely sociable. He loved to take a country house near London for some of the summer months and to have his friends stay with him. Macready, Thomas Mitton, now an established lawyer, John Forster, the novelists Thackeray and Harrison Ainsworth, and the painter Daniel Maclise were among those who visited him.

They were not allowed much rest. Dickens insisted on long walks, and also on every kind of game, running races, jumping matches, cricket, quoits, battledore and shuttlecock, bagatelle, dancing. There was always one of these going on, and whichever it was Dickens threw himself into it with the ardor of a small boy, and generally succeeded for a while at least, in working up his companions to the same enthusiasm.

He was enjoying life enormously. Occasionally a bad review of one of his books would make him angry or sad for an hour. *The Times* especially always attacked his books viciously, but although Dickens was irritated at the time, he soon forgot it. He remarked about his bad reviews, "The good and pleasant things are mixed up with every moment of our existence so plentifully that we scarcely heed them."

Kate Dickens did not take any part in these violent activities. She had two little daughters now as well as her son, young Charles. By the time their second girl was born in 1839, the Dickens' found the house in Doughty Street too small for their family. They moved to No. 1 Devonshire Terrace, a house with a garden and divided only by a road from Regent's Park.

Kate had always been short of energy, and found her young family exhausting. Her sister Georgina Hogarth often came for a long visit to help, and gradually became very much part of the household. Kate needed her all the more because when Dickens was not furiously busy working he was very much occupied with his friends. He was beginning to be asked to the great houses of London, where Kate was not always invited with him. Perhaps it was lucky in some ways that she was independent and preferred a quiet life. It suited her that Charles should go all over the place without her while she with Georgina and the babies stayed peacefully at home.

∼⟨ 10 ⟩∼

THE success of *Nicholas Nickleby* enabled Chapman and Hall to pay Dickens an unexpected £1500 and to offer him £50 a week for a new magazine which he proposed to edit. He was also to have a half share of the profits.

He could now afford to provide a comfortable home for his parents, whom he had been helping all the time. He rushed down to Devonshire and found a charming little country house for his father and mother at Alphington, near Exeter. "It is," he assured John Dickens, "a jewel of a house in the most beautiful, cheerful, delicious rural neighbourhood, and I should love to live there myself if I were older."

John Dickens did not share this enthusiasm. He asked what on earth he was expected to do in a place like Alphington. The truth was that it was necessary for Charles to get his father out of London. John Dickens had developed a habit of going around to his son's pub-

lishers and asking for a loan, implying that Charles had
sent him. He had also started a promising trade in scraps
of his son's handwriting, which he sold to admiring auto-
graph hunters. To Alphington he had to go. Charles fur-
nished the house with everything his parents could want
from carpets and curtains to coal and gardening tools.
They went but John Dickens did not stay there. He was
soon to be heard of traveling around England and running up bills in various towns.

In this year, 1839, Charles Dickens, now twenty-seven
years old, was the most widely read author his country
had ever known. There was no need for him to do anything except sit down and write more novels, but his
energy spilled over, and he was eager about the new
magazine he was to edit. He decided to call it *Master
Humphrey's Clock.* He was haunted by a vision of
lonely people all over the country sitting desolate by
their firesides, in need of a friendly hand and voice,
which he hoped his magazine would supply. He told
John Forster that he had a picture in his mind of "an
old fellow in a curious old house, who had a particular
affection for an old green cased grand father's clock, in
whose case he discovered a lot of old papers about his
early life."

While he was planning the magazine, Dickens suddenly plunged into an absurd fantasy about the young
Queen Victoria, who in February 1840 married her
cousin Prince Albert of Saxe-Coburg-Gotha. Dickens
told everybody that he was madly in love with her, and
that her marriage was a tragedy for him.

"I am utterly lost in misery and can do nothing," he wrote to John Forster. He spoke of drowning himself in the Serpentine, or in the Regent's Canal; of cutting his throat with a razor blade, of falling under the feet of a cab horse. He poured out all this to the older writer, Walter Savage Landor, who was very much upset, because he thought "poor young Charles Dickens" was going off his head. Other people thought this too, especially when Dickens wrote to a friend.

> I have heard on the Lord Chamberlain's authority that the Queen reads my books. I think she may be sorry when I am gone. I should wish to be embalmed, and kept . . . if practicable, on the top of a triumphal arch at Buckingham Palace when She is in town, and on the East turret of the Round Tower when She is at Windsor.

It was a game, of course, but Dickens threw himself into it so wholeheartedly, as he did into any game he was playing, that his puzzled friends did not know whether to take him seriously or not. The nonsense came abruptly to an end when Dickens suddenly realized that the first issue of *Master Humphrey's Clock* was due to appear in two months, and that he had not begun to write the serial he planned for it, which was to be called *The Old Curiosity Shop*.

Dickens wrote to Forster, "I find that it will be necessary to go on a perfect regimen of diet and exercise."

Having sobered himself down in this way he set to work on the first number of *The Old Curiosity Shop*. A novel is always made up of digested experience. What the novelist sees or hears or feels or reads about is absorbed into his mind, where it may be changed, enriched, by what is already there, and reappear in what seems at first sight to be something quite different. A journalist's material is always recognizable. He writes down what he sees. His work is the work of the photographer giving a faithful representation. But the novelist has to lose sight of his material for a time so that his creative imagination can work on it underground. What he produces is not a photograph but a picture, suggested to him by his material. It is the truth of the imagination that informs his work, not necessarily factual truth, and he may find his inspiration anywhere, and transmute it into anything.

The idea of *The Old Curiosity Shop* first came to Dickens when he went to Egham Races, and saw two men showing a Punch and Judy. They were accompanied by "a seedy old man and a little girl in a plain stuff dress, who held the hat."

These two became Little Nell and her grandfather, the two central characters in the novel, but Nell, the gentle, lovely, innocent girl who died young, also embodied all Dickens' deep feeling for the dead Mary Hogarth.

When the book opens Nell is living with her grandfather, Mr. Trent, in the rooms behind the curiosity shop. The old man does not make much money from the shop, and he needs money for he is a secret gambler who steals out at night to play and generally loses. He

LITTLE NELL.

From The Old Curiosity Shop

constantly borrows small sums of money from an evil dwarf, Quilp. Quilp bullies his meek wife, terrifies his neighbors and associates, and rejoices in the fact that by these constant loans, which Mr. Trent has no hope of repaying, he is getting both Grandfather and Little Nell into his power, and will be able to take possession of the shop in payment of the debt.

When Quilp threatens to do this, old Mr. Trent has a serious illness which leaves him weak and childish. As soon as he is fit to walk he and Nell slip away "to fly from this wicked city into the green happy country."

The rambling story of their adventures has the enchantment of a fairy tale. They are first taken in tow by the two owners of a Punch and Judy show; frightened by the rough crowds at a race meeting they slip away from the showman, and come to a village where the schoolmaster takes them into his cottage, and Nell soothes the deathbed of one of his young pupils, "the little scholar."

Leaving the village they are taken in by Mrs. Jarley, the owner of a wax works show, who travels the road in a caravan, stopping at every fair ground. Nell helps by mending the clothes of the wax works and soon learns to show them, but her grandfather's old destroying obsession is upon him again. He steals Nell's money to gamble with. She finds out that he is going to steal Mrs. Jarley's, and takes him away. They wander on again until they come to the village where the schoolmaster has a new post. There he finds refuge for them, but Nell, worn out by her journeys and anxieties, dies.

Dickens was so moved by his own story that he could hardly bear to write this scene. Deeply as he had grieved for Mary Hogarth, the pressing demands of work and family life had obliged him to cut short his mourning. Now all his feelings came out over the death of Little Nell, and for days while he was writing this installment he could go nowhere and see nobody. *The Old Curiosity Shop* would have been a better book if *only* Nell had died. The deathbed of the little scholar as well seems to us now to weaken the tragedy by repetition, but Dickens wrote as he felt at the time, and while writing this book he was working off a great deal of sadness.

There is a gallery of lively minor characters in *The Old Curiosity Shop*, not only those whom Nell and her grandfather meet on their wanderings, but also the riff-raff who surround Quilp; Sampson Brass, the shady lawyer who truckles to him; Sampson's bolder sister, Sally Brass; Dick Swiveller, Sampson's lodger, a charming penniless scapegrace with a saving humanity, and the Marshioness, his own name for the downtrodden little servant of the house whom he befriends, at first with casual kindness, later with real affection.

Quilp, with his high spirits, his dynamic energy, and his taste for playing tricks on people has something of Dickens himself in him, and although Dickens was probably not conscious of this, he gave to the bullied Mrs. Quilp something of the manner and appearance of his own wife, fair, gentle, slow, blue-eyed, timid. Although *The Old Curiosity Shop* has more of the quality of a fairy tale than any other novel by Dickens, perhaps no other book of his except *David Copperfield* contains so much of his own reality, exaggerated and transmuted so as to be almost unrecognizable.

The book was an enormous success. Men and women, even the dour Carlyle, wept over Little Nell. Crowds waiting on the quay in New York shouted out, "Is Little Nell dead?" to the passengers on board the ship that brought over the latest number of *Master Humphrey's Clock.*

⚓ 11 ⚓

In JUNE 1841, Charles and Kate Dickens paid a visit to Scotland. They were entertained at a large public banquet; Dickens was given the freedom of the City of Edinburgh, and received ovations at the theater. His hotel was besieged by reporters and other callers. "I have been forced," he wrote, "to take refuge in a sequestered room at the end of a long passage."

He was also asked to stand for Parliament for a Scottish constituency in the Whig interest. He refused as he had already refused to stand in England for Reading. He knew that for him it would be a waste of time. While he was in Edinburgh he went to see the house where Sir Walter Scott had lived for twenty-seven years. He wrote to Forster after a week of being fêted.

"There is no place like home. I thank God for having given me a quiet spirit and a heart that won't hold many people. I sigh for Devonshire Terrace and Broadstairs, for battledore and shuttlecock (his favorite game of the moment). I want to dine in a blouse with you and Mac."

To those who lived with him it hardly seemed that the ever restless, active Dickens possessed a quiet spirit, but he was soon tired of public occasions, and loved the ease of his home and the casual company of his close friends far better than being lionized.

Vacations, anyhow, could not last long for *Master Humphrey's Clock* had to be kept ticking. Dickens was already at work on another story to be serialized in the magazine. It was the first of his two historical novels. It was called *Barnaby Rudge*, which was a new version of his old idea of a novel to be called *Gabriel Varden, the Locksmith of London*.

The story opens in 1775, and finishes five years later during the Gordon Riots of 1780. Parliament had just brought in a Bill to remove some of the oppressive restrictions on Roman Catholics living in England. Lord George Gordon, who was half mad, raised a cry of "No Popery," and so inflamed the more embittered Prostestants in the country, that they started a week of rioting in London, in which the genuine Protestants were soon joined by all the vagabonds, thugs and thieves in the city.

Against this historical background Dickens sets the story of the explanation of a murder committed some years before the book opens. Gabriel Varden, the sturdy locksmith, of London, around whom Dickens had originally meant to build the novel, is still one of the chief characters, but the central figure of the tale is Barnaby Rudge himself, a poor half-witted youth living with his mother under the shadow of a secret connected with the murder.

Barnaby owns a pet raven, as Dickens himself did at that time. Trailing about with his bird on his shoulder, the poor half-wit is a touchstone for the other characters; the humane and benevolent try to protect him; the vicious involve him in destructive activities which nearly cause his death.

The second half of *Barnaby Rudge,* with its vivid descriptions of that week in London in 1780 when the forces of the law, taken by surprise, were powerless against the mob, is far better than the first half. *Barnaby Rudge* is the book in which Dickens came most near to imitating Scott, for whom he had great admiration. There is much less fun in it than in *Nicholas Nickleby* or in *The Old Curiosity Shop,* but it contains one superbly ludicrous character, Sim Tappertit, Gabriel Varden's apprentice. Sim is an active follower of the crazy Lord George Gordon, and cherishes immense dreams of power and grandeur. Sim is

> in years just twenty, in looks much older, in conceit at least two hundred. He is very small but with an ambitious and aspiring soul. He has majestic shadowy ideas concerning the power of his eye, folds his arms with sullen majesty and behaves in a very mysterious, aloof and awe inspiring manner.

In the odd way in which such things sometimes happen, the character in *Barnaby Rudge* who made the greatest impression on those who read the serial parts as they came out in *Master Humphrey's Clock*, was the locksmith's young daughter, Dolly Varden. All we know about her is that she was enchantingly pretty, wore small hats trimmed with flowers, and didn't have enough sense to know which young man she was in love with. But Dickens described her prettiness and her girlish charm so successfully that his girl readers went about in little hats trimmed with flowers called "Dolly Varden hats" and everyone sang and whistled a popular song:

> Dolly Dolly Dolly Dolly Varden,
> Dresses like a little flowery garden.

Barnaby Rudge appeared in *Master Humphrey's Clock* immediately after *The Old Curiosity Shop*. But the editor was now getting tired of his magazine. He was suffering from an unusually acute fit of restlessness, and began to think that he wanted to see the United States before he was old. He was twenty-nine, but as he looked at his fourth child, born in the Spring of 1841, he exclaimed, "I am expecting every day to be grey and have very nearly persuaded myself that I am gouty."

By the Fall of that year he was obsessed by a wish to go to the United States. "I am haunted by visions of America night and day. Kate cries dismally if I mention the subject, but God willing I think it *must* be managed somehow."

Kate, never adventurous nor energetic, did not want to leave the four children, but Macready and her sister,

Georgina, promised to look after them. Dickens wrote to an American correspondent, "I hope in the third week of the new year to set my foot upon the soil I have trodden in my day dreams many times, and whose sons and daughters I yearn to know and be among."

⌒⟨ 12 ⟩⌒

THE American people were waiting to see Charles
Dickens as eagerly as he was looking forward to meeting them. His books were widely read all over the
United States. To his readers in the comparatively new
Republic he was the son of the people who had raised
himself to eminence by his genius: he was the apostle
of liberty and fraternity; he praised the ordinary man
and satirized stuffy British traditions and institutions.
It did not occur to his enthusiastic American admirers
that a satirist may find a subject for his satire in any
country.

The Britannia docked at Boston on January 22nd,
1842. Dickens was ready to go ashore, "in full fig, a
beaver hat, a brown frock coat, a waistcoat figured in
red, and a large patterned cravat fastened by two diamond pins." Over all this he wore a shaggy fur coat that

he had bought in Regent Street. Though he was just approaching his thirtieth birthday he looked much younger with his pink and white complexion, the long hair curling over his ears, and his large bright eyes that easily filled with tears.

"How can I give you the faintest notion of my reception here," he wrote to Forster, "of the crowds that pour in and out all day; of the people that line the streets when I go out; of the cheering when I went to the theatre; of the copies of verses, letters of congratulations, welcome of all kinds, balls, dinners, assemblies without end. I have had deputations from the far West, who have come more than two thousand miles distance, from the lakes, the rivers, the backwoods, the log-houses, the cities, factories, villages, towns. I have heard from the universities, Congress, Senate, and bodies public and private of every sort and kind." He added, "There was never a king nor emperor upon earth so cheered and followed by crowds."

On the other hand the dignified citizens of Boston were slightly shocked by the two diamond tiepins, and the red patterned waistcoats; their own waistcoats were made of black satin. They thought the young writer too free and easy in his manner and were outraged when he referred to a beautiful woman as "kissable." But these were the more formal and sober members of the community. Dickens remained the idol of the majority, and was praised to the skies by the press until he made his first big speech at a public banquet at Hartford. He began by saying,

I have faith and wish to diffuse faith in existence. I take it that we hold our sympathies and energies in trust for the Many not the Few; that we cannot hold in too strong a light of disgust and contempt all meanness, falsehood, cruelty and oppression, above all that nothing is high because it is in a high place; nothing is low because it is in a low one.

This opening won a tremendous round of applause from the audience but they were not so well pleased with what followed. Dickens proceeded to attack with great vigor the American publishers' habit of "pirating" his books and those of other English writers. In those days there was no international law of copyright protecting the authors' rights to his own work in any country where it was published. Dickens was more widely read in the United States than any other author, and he had not made a penny by it. American publishers seized upon each of his novels as it appeared, printed huge editions, but paid the author nothing. They were doing the same to other English authors. They had done it, as Dickens indignantly remembered, to Sir Walter Scott, who died of overwork because he needed money so badly, and might have been saved by the royalties which American publishers owed him.

The United States was still a very young nation, not a hundred years from the Declaration of Independence. Her citizens, anxious to establish themselves in every way on the map of the world, were acutely sensitive to criticism. They had made an image of Dickens as an un-

*Charles Dickens delivering a speech on his first
visit to the United States*

worldly man of ideals, almost a saint: they were outraged that he should stand up at a public dinner given in his honor and demand the money that was owed him and his fellow authors. The American Press turned against Dickens, calling him "a mercenary scoundrel" and other names. They attacked him from the Hartford banquet to the end of his visit.

But nothing could stop his triumphal progress. When he went to the theater in New York audiences sprang to their feet and burst into applause as "Mr. Dickens and his lady" took their seats. When he came back at night from a banquet or a reception there were always several hundred people waiting at his hotel to shake hands with him. He was never left alone for a minute. Only the presence of Kate protected him at all from the admiring women who thronged around him.

"If I had not a lady with me," he wrote to Forster, "I should be obliged to fly the country!" It is not surprising that after about a fortnight of this he was lying in a state of near-collapse on a sofa in a hotel, with Kate weeping by his side. He recovered and they both went to a great ball in the Park Theater, New York. Charles was wearing a black suit and a gay waistcoat, Kate in white figured Irish tabinet, with a blue wreath in her fair hair and blue ribbons to match her eyes.

Everybody watched them as they danced the first cotillion together. The general opinion was that Kate was smartly dressed but not really smart; she was very quiet, and seemed to accept all the homage with resignation. Dickens they thought "bright eyed and intelligent looking, brash in manners, lively in talk, somewhat of a dandy with rings and things."

There was another huge banquet at which Washington Irving took the chair, and with great tact proposed a toast to "Mr. Dickens and International Copyright," which forestalled both Dickens and the critics who were waiting for him. Dickens enjoyed meeting his fellow authors more than anything else. He made great friends with Longfellow who soon came over to England to stay with him. He met Edgar Allan Poe, who at that time was hardly recognized even in his own country. Dickens took Poe's short stories back to London and tried to find an English publisher for them, but was unsuccessful.

The triumphal progress continued to Philadelphia where Dickens, after shaking hands for two hours with a stream of visitors, exclaimed when yet another was presented to him as "one of the most remarkable men of our country." "Good God! They are all so!" This scene he later reproduced in his novel *Martin Chuzzlewit*.

In Washington Dickens was received by President Tyler, and listened to a debate in the Senate, where the men struck him as much more remarkable than their speeches. He visited Richmond, Charleston, and other cities in the South, as well as Pittsburgh, Cincinnati, and St. Louis. Here Dickens spoke vehemently against slavery. Not only his stand on slavery but his clothes, which were considered flashy, aroused a great deal of feeling against him in the South.

The American tour finished with a visit to Niagara Falls, which curiously reminded Dickens of Mary Hogarth, because the sight and sound of the falls moved him to solemn feelings. He and Katie spent a week at Niagara "to our unspeakable delight, without company," and then went on into Canada, where they stayed in Montreal as the guests of the Coldstream Guards. Here Dickens enjoyed a treat after his own heart, stage-managing and producing two plays in the regimental theatricals. All the same both he and Kate were homesick, and she could hardly bear to look at Maclise's portrait of their four children which was set up every night in their suite.

On June 7th they started on the journey back to them, embarking on a sailing ship from New York. On June 29th they arrived home late in the evening and Dickens pulled all four children out of bed to hug them and romp with them, which made them so excited that one of them went into convulsions.

13

BEFORE going to the United States Dickens had promised a travel book and a new novel to his publishers. As soon as he had settled down at home he began to write the travel book, which he called *American Notes*. He relied a good deal on his always vivid memory, but he also used some of the long letters he had written to Forster describing the town.

American Notes is as nearly dull as a book by Dickens can be. He wrote mostly about his visits to public institutions, such as hospitals, prisons, orphanages, and deaf and dumb asylums. He thought that on the whole these compared favorably with their counterparts in England; for instance "Charity Children" in the United States did not wear uniforms and seemed to him to be less regimented than children in English orphanages.

Dickens admitted that there were many slave-owners in America who treated their slaves with great kindness,

but he emphasized by a number of true stories how entirely the slaves were at the mercy of masters who had
no conscience. Children were sold away from their parents, husbands were compelled to beat their wives, preg-
nant women were lashed by overseers to make them
work harder up to the very day of their children's birth.

Some people said that public opinion would be against
such treatment, but, Dickens pointed out, public opinion
had allowed these things to happen. It was utterly wrong
that any man should own any other man as a possession.
While human nature remained fallible, human beings
could not be trusted with so much power over others.
He concluded the book with a vigorous attack on slavery.
Longfellow, who was now in England staying with
Dickens, thought *American Notes* "both good natured
and severe," but the attack on slavery "grand."

The historian and essayist Thomas Macaulay, who was
asked to review *American Notes* for *The Edinburgh Review*, sent the book back to the Editor. "I have eaten
salt with Dickens," he wrote, "a good man and a man
of real talent. I cannot praise this book and I will not
cut it up." The truth was that Dickens, the reporter, had
long ago been displaced by Dickens the novelist. He said
what he wanted to say about the United States with far
more conviction, vitality, and prejudice in a few chapters
of his next novel, *Martin Chuzzlewit*.

Dickens had the greatest difficulty in starting *Martin
Chuzzlewit*, perhaps because he had enjoyed such a long
holiday from writing fiction. For days he shut himself
up in his room and could not put a word on paper. He

remarked that when he emerged he was "so horribly cross and surly that the boldest fly at my approach." Nearly every imaginative writer finds himself at some time in this situation. As usually happens, the inner resistance gave way in the end, and Dickens was at last able to write the first installment.

His purpose in *Martin Chuzzlewit* was "to show by more or less every person introduced the number and variety of humors that have their roots in selfishness."

There are two Martin Chuzzlewits in the novel, Old Martin is a rich man who suspects, on the whole rightly, that all his family are hanging around him in the hope of inheriting some of his money. His grandson, another Martin Chuzzlewit, is, when the book opens, a brash, egotistical young man without a thought for other people.

Old Martin has adopted and trained as his companion a young girl, Mary Graham. The old man has made it perfectly clear to Mary that she is to expect nothing after his death, and so hopes to prevent her from looking forward to it. Mary is a mild, gentle, colorless girl, hardly more than a peg in the story.

Dickens is probably the genius next to Shakespeare in the hierarchy of English letters. Like Shakespeare he has a gallery of rich characters, villains, rogues and comics. But he could never have created a Rosalind, or Viola. There is no girl of wit and spirit in his novels. They are all mild, colorless, submissive, and Mary Graham has even less character than most of them.

Young Martin is apprenticed to a cousin of the Chuzzlewits, Seth Pecksniff, who runs a training school for architects in a West Country town, and does very well out of it by charging them fees, and selling their best designs as his own. Mr. Pecksniff, meant to be the prime incarnation of selfishness in the book, is so tremendous and amusing a humbug that the reader almost likes him, and certainly welcomes his appearance in any chapter.

Martin Chuzzlewit has a more complicated plot than the earlier novels. There is another cousin, Jonas Chuzzlewit, as sinister a villain as Dickens ever created, who plans the murder of his old father, and finally does murder an associate in some shady business, and who knows enough about Jonas to be dangerous to him. The scenes leading up to the murder are among the most dramatic passages that Dickens ever wrote.

This sub-plot is also linked to the main story by Jonas' marriage to Mr. Pecksniff's younger daughter, Mercy, who accepts him in a fit of giddy triumph over her elder sister, Charity, and suffers cruelly as a result of her folly. Young Martin falls in love with Mary Graham, and old Martin, who wants all her attention for himself, is furiously angry.

Old Martin makes a parade of friendship with Pecksniff, and persuades him to send young Martin away. Martin, with Mark Tapley, the bartender from the nearby inn, goes off to the United States to try and make his fortune.

The chapters of *Martin Chuzzlewit* which describe young Martin's American adventures aroused a good deal of indignation at that time in the United States. As when

MARTIN CHUZZLEWIT.

BY

CHARLES DICKENS.

Philadelphia:

T. B. PETERSON, No. 306 CHESTNUT STREET.

he wrote of the English Parliament and the English Law, so when he wrote of the American life and the American people, Dickens saw with a keen eye what was wrong and absurd, and left out or took for granted much that was good and useful. He had been sharply criticized himself in the United States, and he did not see why they should resent being criticized in return. "We must be cracked up, Sir," said one American character in *Martin Chuzzlewit.* "You are not now in a despotic land. We air a model to the earth and we must be cracked up, I tell you."

Martin is persuaded in New York to buy with what little money he has "an estate" in a district called Eden. The estate turns out to be an awful, fever ridden swamp. Martin's sufferings there, and still more the example of Mark Tapley's courage, and persistent devotion . . . (how irritating Mark's incessant cheerfulness is to the modern reader!) . . . bring home to the spoiled young man the fact that he is not the center of the universe, and has much to learn from his servant. He returns to England penniless and disappointed, but nearer to manhood. Meanwhile in alternate chapters Dickens keeps the English part of the narrative going, and enriches it with other characters.

Pecksniff, bland, sanctimonious, with a sharp eye all the time on self interest, is a masterpiece, but hardly less of a masterpiece is Sarah Gamp, "Sairey," a satirical portrait of the professional nurse of the days before Florence Nightingale taught the necessity for real training, and raised the status of the profession.

She was a fat old woman, this Mrs. Gamp, with a husky voice and a moist eye, which she had a remarkable power of turning up and showing the white of it. Having very little neck it cost her some trouble to look over herself at those to whom she talked. The face of Mrs. Gamp, the nose particularly, was somewhat red and swollen and it was difficult to enjoy her society without becoming conscious of the swell of spirits.

Mrs. Gamp has an imaginary patient, a Mrs. Harris into whose mouth she puts all the things that she would like to say or hear said about herself.

If it wasn't for the nerve a little sip of liquor gives me . . . I was never able to do more than taste it . . . I never could go through with what I sometimes has to do. "Mrs. Harris," I says, "leave the bottle on the chimley piece and don't ask me to take none, but let me put my lips to it when so dispoged and then I will do what I am engaged to do according to the best of my ability." "Mrs. Gamp," Mrs. Harris says in answer, "if ever there was a sober creature to be got at eighteen pence a day for working people and three and six for gentle folks—nightwatching," said Mrs. Gamp with emphasis, being an extra charge . . . "you are that invallable person." "Mrs. Harris," I says to her, "don't name the charge for if I could afford to lay out my fellow creatures for nothing I would gladly do it such is the love I bear them."

Mrs. Gamp has a friend and colleague, Betsy Prigg, with whom she often shares a night watch over a patient. They relieve the tedium of their watch by sharing "the bottle on the chimley piece" and as large a salad as the green grocer can get into Mrs. Gamp's pocket for sixpence. But even the close alliance of the two nurses breaks down when Betsy Prigg, tired of hearing Mrs. Harris quoted so often as a testimony to the virtues of Sarah Gamp, exclaims, "Bother Mrs. Harris. I don't believe there's no sich a person!" After the utterances of which expression she leaned forward and snapped her fingers once twice thrice each time nearer to the face of Mrs. Gamp.

"What!" said Mrs. Gamp. "You bage creetur! Have I knowed Mrs. Harris five and thirty year to be told at last that there ain't such a person living? Have I stood her friend in all her troubles great and small, for it to come at last to sech an end as this?" It is the final insult, worse than the night when Mrs. Prigg seized the brandy bottle out of Mrs. Gamp's hand and exclaimed, "No, No, Sairey! Drink fair whatever you do."

Todgers, the boarding house in London where Mr. Pecksniff and his daughters stay occasionally, provides Dickens with a cluster of amusing characters brilliantly sketched. It is here that Charity Pecksniff, disappointed, luckily for her, with Jonas, discovers Augustus Moddle, a young man of such mild and defenseless character that she is able to force him to become engaged to her. As the day arranged for the wedding draws near, the shrinking Augustus is out walking with Tom Pinch, Mr. Pecksniff's old assistant. Pinch is a distressingly meek character, one of the few representations of unselfishness in the book in which it must be admitted that the unselfish are presented with far less energy and conviction than the selfish.

> "I wonder," Tom Pinch observed, "that in these crowded streets foot passengers are not oftener run over."
> Mr. Moddle with a dark look replied, "The drivers won't do it."
> "Do you mean?" Tom inquired.
> "That there are some men," replied Mr. Moddle with a hollow laugh, "who *can't* get run over. They live a charmed life. Coal waggons recoil from them; cabs refuse to run them down." "Ah," said Augustus, marking Tom's astonishment, "there are such men. One of them is a friend of mine."

However, Augustus Moddle does manage to escape from Charity's clutch, by sailing on the wedding day to South Africa. The letter which he sends back to her concludes:

> Farewell. Be the proud bride of a ducal coronet, and forget me. Long may it be before you know the anguish with which I now subscribe myself, amid the tempestuous howlings of the—sailors.
> Unalterably never yours,
> Augustus Moddle.

The troubles of the few unselfish characters and of the now reformed young Martin are resolved in the end by

Old Martin Chuzzlewit, who turns out to have been acting a part all the time while he has appeared to trust Pecksniff and to submit to his influence. The good are suitably rewarded, and Pecksniff becomes "a drunken squalid begger-letter-writing man with a shrewish daughter." Dickens was a resolute moralist. Humbugs and exploiters must be punished, even if the reader is almost too grateful for the amusement provided by Pecksniff to want to see him so reduced.

At first *Martin Chuzzlewit* was not a success with Dickens' regular readers. The sales of each installment dropped and the publishers, Chapman and Hall, were worried. Although the sales rose with the introduction of Mrs. Gamp as the sales of Pickwick had risen with the introduction of Sam Weller, they did not reach the heights of the former novels. The reception of *Martin Chuzzlewit* in the United States was naturally resentful and furious. Dickens made less money on the book all around than he had expected, but he was convinced that *Martin Chuzzlewit* was his best novel so far. This conviction and his natural gaiety and courage sustained him under what was a very serious reversal. He wanted to change publishers, particularly since they made him repay the difference between the money they had advanced him and the money earned by the book. They were entitled to do this by a clause in the contract, but it did not pay them in the long run to enforce it!

$\backsim\!\!\prec\! 14 \!\succ\!\backsim$

WHILE he was still writing *Martin Chuzzlewit*, Dickens was suddenly possessed by an idea for a short Christmas story called *A Christmas Carol*.

This is one of the most shapely things that he ever wrote. It opens on Christmas Eve when the mean and curmudgeonly Scrooge, leaving his office without a kind word to his clerk, Bob Cratchitt, or to the nephew who has called to wish him a merry Christmas, walks home to his lonely house and there sees the ghost of his dead partner, Marley, who warns him to expect a visitation at midnight.

On the stroke of twelve, Scrooge is visited by the first of three ghosts: the Ghost of Christmas Past, who recalls to him the scenes of his boyhood when he was still able to love and feel; the Ghost of Christmas Present follows, who shows him how Bob Cratchitt and his family, and his nephew and others are rejoicing in the season; and

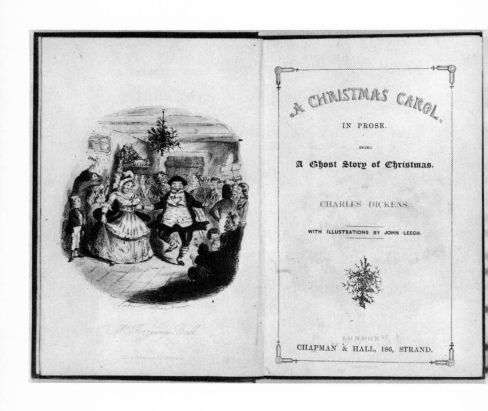

Illustration by John Leech. From the "Experimental" edition of 1844

the Ghost of Christmas Future shows him his own death
—alone and unloved, tended only by those who rob him
as soon as life is out of his body. Scrooge awakens on the
real Christmas morning to find that there is still time to
revive the feelings of the past, to give pleasure to others
in the present and to change the future.

Dickens was wildly excited by this story. He "wept
and laughed and wept again" as he wrote it. While working on it he "walked about the black streets of London
fifteen and twenty miles many a night, when all sober
folks had gone to bed." The story was immediately popular with his readers but owing to the unsatisfactory
contract which Forster had arranged for him with Chapman and Hall, Dickens made very little money out of
the book. Part of the trouble was that Forster was now
literary adviser to Chapman and Hall, and he favored
the publishers in the contract at the expense of the author.

Dickens by now had five children, Charley, Mary or
Mamie, Katie, Walter, Landor, and Francis Jeffery. He
was also supporting his father and mother, and helping
his brother Fred. He began to find himself very hard up.
He saw that he ought to be getting more money for his
books so he decided to break with his present publishers
Chapman and Hall. It was too difficult to do this through
John Forster since he was on their staff, so Dickens arranged it through his old friend Thomas Mitton, now a
successful lawyer, who made a contract for the next
book with Bradbury and Evans.

Then suddenly Dickens decided to go and live abroad.
He thought it would be cheaper if only because it would

Charles Dickens reading to his daughters. Drawing after a contemporary photograph

put a stop to his endless hospitality to the large number of his friends in London. He knew that he would not be capable of cutting this down so long as he stayed in the same city. He so much loved seeing people, he was so generous to his friends that he could not meet one of them in the street without asking him to dinner. In Italy where he would know nobody he could get along more quietly with his work, and live more economically.

By way of beginning the economy he gave a splendid farewell dinner party for all his best friends. Next he bought a big traveling coach which needed four horses to draw it. Charley Dickens, who was then seven years old, always remembered walking uphill on the French roads when they got out to lighten the load for the horses, and hearing their ninety-six bells jingling behind him.

The house which they had rented in advance, Villa Bella Vista, or the House of the Beautiful View, was in Albarro, a suburb of Genoa. It proved to be disappointing; the lane leading to it was overgrown, the gardens were neglected; the hall looked like a cellar, the marble staircase was cracked, and lizards, rats, scorpions, fleas and flies infested the disused rooms. Dickens called the place "the Pink Jail."

It was July when they arrived, and by the end of September they had forgotten about economizing. They left the Villa Bella Vista and established themselves in another and much better house in Genoa itself. It was called the Palazzo Peschiere, the Palace of the Fishponds, and it looked down over a sweetly scented garden to a spreading view of Genoa. But even here living abroad was not a great success. Dickens found that he could not write in Genoa. For one thing the constant noise of the bells from the city churches drove him mad. Kate was unhappy because Dickens started trying to cure a neighbor, Mrs. De La Rue, of nervous delusions by hypnotizing her, for which he believed himself to have a gift. It seemed to poor Kate that if her husband spent so much time and thought on Mrs. De La Rue he must be in love with her.

The bells had their uses after all, and the excitement of trying to hypnotize Mrs. De La Rue palled, when in October Dickens was inspired by the noisy chimes of Genoa to write a Christmas short story about London bells called *The Chimes*. It is a sketch of a ticket porter called Trotty Veck, who sees a terrifying vision of his daughter's future and cries out to the spirit of the bells to save her.

Dickens thought of the story as "a blow struck for the poor" since it was her desperate poverty that was going to drive Trotty Veck's daughter to her ruin!

"I am in a regular, ferocious excitement about *The Chimes*," he wrote to Forster, "I get up at seven; have a cold bath, before breakfast, and blaze away wrathful, and red and hot until 3 p.m. or so when I usually knock off for the day."

"I have had a good cry," he wrote as he came to the end of the story. "I am worn to death. I was obliged to lock myself in yesterday, for my face was swollen for the time to twice its proper size, and was hugely ridiculous."

One of the disadvantages of living abroad now became clear to Dickens since he wanted at once to show his new story to Forster and to read it aloud to his friends. He rushed off to London, sightseeing on the way at a pace that exhausted his couriers. Forster was waiting for him, and had arranged a dinner party for a choice band of great friends who, after a good dinner, sat around the fire in Forster's room and heard the first reading of *The Chimes*.

Dickens always loved this story. "The intensity of it," Forster said, "seemed always best to represent what he hoped to be remembered for." It has never enjoyed the wide popularity of *The Christmas Carol*.

On his way back to Italy, Dickens stopped in Paris where his actor friend Macready was playing in a short season of Shakespeare and other plays. Dickens plunged happily into the society of French actors and writers. He met among others Theophile Gautier, Victor Hugo, and Alexandre Dumas. He hurried on through a snow storm to join his family at Genoa for Christmas. He wrote to Mrs. Macready.

"I was so cold after leaving you and dear Macready in Paris that I was taken out of the coach at Marseilles in a perfectly torpid state, and was at first supposed to be luggage, but the porters, not being able to find any directions upon me, led to a further examination and what the newspapers call, 'the vital spark,' was finally discovered under a remote corner of the travelling shawls."

He reached Genoa in time for Christmas, where the

Dickens family made a sensation with an iced cake weighing ninety pounds which Angela Burdett Coutts had sent her godson, Charley. The cake had to go to a confectioners to have its sugar ornaments repaired after the journey, and all the shop's customers came to admire its bonbons and crackers and "Twelfth Night" figures.

As soon as Christmas was over, Dickens and his wife went off to see Rome. It was not a city in which Dickens felt at home, he had no sympathy with the Catholic Church and not much knowledge of ancient history. He went back to Genoa, but still found himself unable to write anything except his *Pictures of Italy*, which Bradbury and Evans were only too eager to publish. In June Dickens gave up for the time being the attempt to live abroad, and brought his family back to London.

Here he made another dive into journalism. He had always been afraid of being forced, like Walter Scott, to write more novels than he could write well because of financial necessity. He often tried some other way of earning a living for a short time. He undertook now to edit a new Liberal paper, the *Daily News*.

The first number was published on January 21, 1846. In February, Dickens resigned the editorship. No one knows exactly what happened, whether he suddenly realized that he was not going to have as free a hand as he hoped, or whether he felt that he was going to be too tied to the office, Dickens himself said that his editorship had been "a brief mistake." Probably the real reason was that he had a new novel in mind, for he went off to Lausanne with his family and began *Dombey and Son*.

Dombey and Son was intended "to do for pride what *Martin Chuzzlewit* had done for selfishness."

Mr. Dombey is a London merchant, whose pride is in his firm, and whose chief ambition is to have a son who will eventually come into partnership with him so that the firm, in which Mr. Dombey used to be a partner with his father, will really again be Dombey and Son. This overriding ambition makes Mr. Dombey indifferent if not actually hostile to the daughter, Florence, who is his first-born child. She cannot be of any use to Dombey and Son.

The longed-for son Paul is born when Florence is six years old. His mother dies at his birth. Little Paul, growing up in the stately cold household, gives all his love to Florence who mothers him. He shows an early distrust of his father's preoccupation with money-making. Sitting in his small chair by his father's great one in front of the fire, little Paul asks,

"Papa, what is money?"
Mr. Dombey was quite disconcerted.
"What is money, Paul," he answered, "Money?"
"Yes," said the child laying his hands on the arms of his chair and turning up an old face to Mr. Dombey. "What is money?"
Mr. Dombey would have liked to give him some explanation, involving the terms, circulating—medium, currency . . . bullion, rates of exchange, value of precious metals in the market and so forth; but looking down at the little chair and seeing what a long way down it was he answered,

"Gold and silver and copper. Guineas, shillings and half-pence. You know what they are?"

"Oh yes, I know what they are," said Paul. "I don't mean that, Papa. I mean what's money after all? I mean Papa, what can it do?"

"Money, Paul, can do everything," Mr. Dombey replies.

Paul counters with the unanswerable question, "Why didn't money save me my Mamma?"

Money cannot save Paul either. Always a delicate child, he dies young in a scene which moved all Dickens' readers to tears, and caused Thackeray to exclaim, "There is no writing against such power as this. One has no chance." Paul dies in the fifth chapter of the book. One of his friends said to Dickens, "what are you going to do with the other fifteen chapters?"

What he did was to shift the interest to Florence, who continues to love her father and to long for his love through years of coldness and neglect, through his second marriage which fails to give him the son he longs for and ends in disaster, until at last old Dombey, broken and repentant, is left clinging to the daughter whom he always rejected, and to her little girl who reminds him of the child Florence he used to despise.

The theme of *Dombey and Son* is not only pride but that contrast between warmth and coldness of heart which is the real substance of so much of Dickens' work.

Florence has no more spirit nor personality than most of the young girls in Dickens' other novels. We realize now that it would be impossible for her to have no hard feelings at all about the father who treats her so badly. But like so many of these colorless girls, she represents the loving against the unloving, and so our sympathies are with her. In spite of Florence's lack of personality the story is enthralling. *Dombey and Son* is a great novel, richly filled as usual with comic minor characters. Major Bagstock stalks about the streets of Brighton trying to ingratiate himself with the rich Mr. Dombey, by flattery.

"The name of Dombey," said the Major. "It's a great name. It's a name Sir," said the Major firmly, as if he defied Mr. Dombey to contradict him, and would feel it his duty to bully him if he did, "a name that is known and honored in the British possessions abroad. It is a name Sir, that a man is proud to recognize. There is nothing adulatory, Sir, about Joseph Bagstock." His Royal Highness the Duke of York observed on more than one occasion, "There is no adulation in Joey. He is a plain old soldier is Joe. He is tough to a fault is Joseph. But sly, Sir, devilish sly."

Little Paul, sent to Brighton for sea air, lodges in the house of the formidable Mrs. Pipchin, whose husband had broken his heart pumping water out of the Peruvian silver mines. Mrs. Pipchin feeds on chops, sweetbreads and buttered toast while her boarders are fed mostly on vegetables and bread and butter. Paul, an odd, thoughtful child, is not afraid of Mrs. Pipchin. Once when he is staring at her with solemn interest she asks him what he is thinking about.

"You," said Paul without the least reserve.

"And what are you thinking about me?" asked Mrs. Pipchin.

"I was thinking how old you must be," said Paul.

"You mustn't say such things, young gentleman," returned the Dame, "that will never do."

"Why not?" asked Paul.

"Because it's not polite," said Mrs. Pipchin snappishly.

"It's not polite," said Paul, "to eat all the mutton-chops and toast, Wickham says."

"Wickham," retorted Mrs. Pipchin, coloring, "is a wicked, impudent, bold-faced hussy."

"What's that?" inquired Paul.

"Never you mind, Sir," retorted Mrs. Pipchin, "remember the story of the little boy that was gored to death by a mad bull for asking questions."

"If the bull was mad," said Paul, "how did he know that the boy had asked questions? Nobody can go and whisper secrets to a mad bull. I don't believe that story."

There are also old Sol Gills, the instrument-maker, whose nephew Walter Gay works in Mr. Dombey's office and eventually marries Florence Sol Gills' nautical friend, Captain Cuttle, who tries to borrow money for Gills from Mr. Dombey, offering his silver watch, teaspoons and sugar tongs and even his annuity of a hundred a year as security. There is Florence's maid, Susan Nipper, sharp-tongued and kind-hearted, and Florence's half-witted but devoted suitor Mr. Toots, with his instructor in Life, the Game Chicken, who

From Dombey & Son

teaches Mr. Toots to box, by knocking him about the head three times a week for the small consideration of ten and six per visit. The story of *Dombey and Son* is a sad one until the end, for Florence is long in finding happiness, and Mr. Dombey's second marriage ends in tragedy for his wife, Edith, who shows Florence great kindness. All the same the book is full of fun, the kind of humor that is based on a deep underlying humanity.

The English critic Dr. F. R. Leavis wrote in the *Sewanee Review* that *Dombey and Son* is full of an inexhaustibly wonderful poetic life and reinforces the proposition that in the "Victorian age, the poetic strength of the English language goes into the novel, and that the great novelists are the successors to Shakespeare."

Dickens wrote most of *Dombey and Son* in Paris, where he felt better able to work than in the comparative quiet of Lausanne. He liked a capital city with plenty of life going on around him. He rented a very odd-looking sort of house in the Faubourg St. Honoré: "Something," he said, "between a baby house, a shades, a haunted castle and a mad kind of clock, and not to be imagined by the mind of man." It was quite cold in Paris that winter and it cost Dickens a small fortune in firewood, and even then the house could not be properly heated. Besides, he couldn't find a place in it where he could settle down comfortably to write. But he could not really settle down to live and write abroad. He came back to England in time for a grand Dombey Dinner on April 11, 1848, which celebrated the publication of the last installment.

⤳ 15 ⤳

As soon as he had finished *Dombey and Son*, Dickens, always eager for a change from novel writing, organized an amateur theatrical company, with which he gave over sixty performances for charity in London and in the provinces during the next ten years. He managed the company, produced the plays and often acted in them. He found this very satisfying recreation. Once a friend asked him what his most cherished daydream was. He replied, "to settle down for the remainder of my life within easy distance of a great theater in the *direction* of which I should hold supreme authority."

In the next year Dickens also started a magazine called *Household Words*. One of his earliest and most valued contributors was Mrs. Gaskell, whose first novel *Mary Barton* had appeared in 1847. The magazine went well, and *Dombey and Son* sold much better than *Martin Chuzzlewit* so Dickens was less worried about money.

But of course he could not and did not really want to keep away very long from writing novels. As soon as Dombey was published in book form he planned and began to write one of his best and most famous novels, *David Copperfield*.

Dickens had already tried to write his autobiography, but he found it so painful to describe the unhappy part of his early years that on his wife's advice he gave it up. But the material was waiting in his mind to be used, and it was probably because of this that he began to write *David Copperfield* in the first person, David telling his own story.

Soon after he had begun the book Dickens realized that he could use his memories of his own childhood. David, like Dickens, finds the pile of dusty novels in an attic and rapturously enters that world of the imagination. There are episodes from Dickens' own school life in *David Copperfield*. A genial caricature of his father appears in the superb Mr. Micawber, who, like John Dickens, is always on the edge of ruin and always hoping for something to turn up. Like John Dickens he maintains a surprising cheerfulness most of the time, alternating with occasional fits of despair. "I have known him come home to supper with a flood of tears, and a declaration that nothing was now left but jail, and go to bed making a calculation of the expense of putting bow windows in the house 'in case anything turned up'."

Mrs. Micawber, who shares her husband's despairs and his casual optimism, is also a little like Mrs. Dickens, although Charles had already used some of his mother's characteristics for Mrs. Nickleby.

"Talent," observes Mrs. Micawber, "Mr. Micawber has. Capital Mr. Micawber has not," and on another occasion, "With the exception of a heel of Dutch cheese . . . which is not adapted to the wants of a young family . . . there is really not a scrap of anything in the larder. I was accustomed to speak of the larder when I lived with Papa and Mama, but I use the word almost unconsciously. What I mean to express is that there is nothing left to eat in the house."

Dickens, of course, as he said to Forster, made *David Copperfield* "a complicated weaving of truth and fiction." David is based on Dickens' memories of himself as a child but his circumstances are different. His father dies before he is born, and his father's aunt, Betsy Trotwood, who comes to take his mother and her child under her protection because she is certain that the child will be a girl, goes off in dudgeon when she finds that the child is a boy. David's mother marries again, and David's stepfather, the sinister and gloomy Murdstone, sends the boy to a blacking warehouse after his mother's death.

In the chapters about David while he is working in the Blacking Warehouse and lodging with the Micawbers, Dickens told to the world for the first time the story of that period in his life which he still felt so painfully that he had been obliged to give up writing about it in the autobiography. It was ended for the young

Charles Dickens by his father coming out of prison, but David, when the Micawbers leave London in the hope of something turning up somewhere else, runs away to his unknown aunt, and in her care, begins with a relief that the reader feels in every nerve, to lead the happier life of a schoolboy with a good home behind him. Betsy Trotwood is a magnificent character with her sharp tongue, her generous heart, and her secret trouble.

In *David Copperfield* Dickens revived another part of his early life. David, just grown up, and articled to a Mr. Spenlow, a solicitor working in the Doctors' Commons, meets and falls headlong in love with Mr. Spenlow's young daughter, Dora.

Dickens drew Dora from Maria Beadnell, with one important difference. Dora returns David's love, marries him and is only parted from him by her early death. She has the responsive, faithful heart that Maria Beadnell lacked. But she also has the exquisite prettiness, the childish charm, the silliness that is lovable in her because she is affectionate and not just a cold-hearted flirt as her prototype was. It is as though in this book Dickens relived his old strong feeling for Maria, and soothed his deep sense of hurt by making Dora give to David what Maria could not give to him.

Yet Dickens knew, too, that he could not have been fully satisfied with Maria. David loves his "child wife" whom Betsy Trotwood calls "Little Blossom," but the fact that she cannot grow out of her childishness worries him. He makes the unsuccessful attempt to form her mind which on his aunt's advice he abandons since it only distresses Dora. He has to learn to accept her as she is. There is a moving passage where he ponders some words that he has heard spoken about another unsuitable marriage.

"There can be no disparity in marriage like unsuitability of mind and purpose . . . the first mistaken impulse of an undisciplined heart." It is the moment when David sees his mistake and knows that he must learn to live with it, but it is also Dickens' comment on the dream of Maria Beadnell, which had lingered in the back of his mind for so many years. Perhaps it is also a comment on his marriage. Writers are lucky, especially novelists. They can use their losses, their mistakes, and their disappointments creatively, for with pen and paper they can exorcise their ghosts.

There is another story running through *David Copperfield*, which links David's nurse, Peggotty, with her brother's family, fishermen who live in a boat connected with a house on a beach at Yarmouth. With the skill of the born storyteller, Dickens connects the child of this family, Little Emily, with the friend whom David makes at school, the brilliant, rudderless, James Steerforth, spoiled son of a doting mother, who for the gratification of his passing whims ruins more than one innocent life.

David Copperfield, especially the first half of it, is a masterpiece. The warm happiness of the little boy at home with his loving mother and nurse, the acute sufferings of the child thrown upon the world, the ardor of friendship, the first fresh experiences of young manhood, the sweetness of early love, all are beautifully described, exquisitely moving and true.

As usual there are crowds of minor characters, many

Illustration from Charles Dickens' David Copperfield.
Mr. Micawber and his family. "I will never desert Mr.
Micawber"

of them as amusing as any that Dickens ever drew. There are unforgettable scenes. There are some weaknesses— as always in any novel by Dickens they are weaknesses of sentimentality, or of a too ready acceptance of the conventions of the Victorian Age. But there are few English novels as good as *David Copperfield*. Thackeray, when he read it, exclaimed generously, "Who can rival this great genius!" And Matthew Arnold wrote of it some years later,

"What a pleasure to have the opportunity of praising a work so sound, a work so rich in merit. What treasure of gaiety, invention, life are in that book! What alertness and resource! What a soul of good nature and kindness governing the whole!"

⚘ 16 ⚘

In the early Spring of 1861, Dickens was busy preparing his theatrical company to give a performance before Queen Victoria. While he was in the middle of this, his father died. Dickens mourned for him sincerely; he had always been fond of him and in the last years had come to respect him. "The longer I live the better man I think him," he said.

Only a few days after this Dickens spent an hour playing with his five-month-old daughter, Dora, and then went off to speak at a public dinner in aid of the General Theatrical Fund, which had been founded to help actors and actresses in difficulties. While he was speaking the news was brought to Forster that Dora had died suddenly, and he had to break this to his friend.

Dickens was much saddened by these two losses. He was a very affectionate father, especially fond of his children when they were small babies. He gave them all nicknames, Mary or Mamie was "Mild Glo'ster" because she was shy and gentle; Katie was "Lucifer Box" because of her quick temper. Walter was called "Young Skull" because of his high cheekbones. The boys, except for Charles the eldest, were all named after Dickens' writer friends. Walter Landor was followed by Francis Jeffery, nicknamed "Chickenstalker." Alfred D'Orsay Tennyson was burdened with the nickname of "Sampson Brass," the rascally lawyer in *The Old Curiosity Shop*. Sydney Smith was "The Ocean Spectre," because of the faraway look in his eyes. Henry Fielding was known as the "Jolly Post Boy," and later Edward Bulwer Lytton became "Plornish" or "Ploon" or even "Plornish Maroontigoonter."

Dickens loved reading to them and playing with them when they were small. He made up stories and sang songs. The children remembered the wonderful Christmas parties he organized for them. At these he gave conjuring performances—Dickens was quite a good conjuror—and danced and pulled crackers, and put on a magic lantern show.

Once when Mamie and Katie had taught him the polka, he woke up at night and was suddenly afraid that he might have forgotten the step. He jumped out of bed and began practising it on his bedroom floor. The next day at the Christmas party he polkaed until he had danced everyone else to a state of exhaustion.

In spite of his grief for his father and Dora, in spite of all his hard work in the theater, Dickens by the Fall of that year, 1861, was "wild to begin a new book." Although he often thought that he wanted to escape from novel writing, he never broke away from it for more than a few months without being in a fever to get back to it.

But first he had to find another larger house for his continually growing family. Perhaps, too, he liked moving because his restlessness was always so acute that he enjoyed any change.

He moved his family in November to Tavistock House in Tavistock Square, Bloomsbury, a charming house with one huge studio room which Dickens thought would make a very good amateur theater. The house was surrounded by a garden. Dickens himself chose carpets, curtains, tables, and mirrors, planed bookcases, and organized the move. Kate Dickens, who did not care for exertion, certainly had a husband who was willing to spare her a good deal of it.

As soon as they were settled in the new home, Dickens began to write *Bleak House*, sometimes working at home and sometimes in a hotel at Broadstairs, a small seaside town on the east coast of Kent, where he liked to go for fresh air and quiet when, as so often happened, he felt the need of a change.

There were times when Dickens lost his temper with his children. He enjoyed his sons' company more when they were little boys than when they were older, and as they grew up they were often frightened of him. But they always knew that his temper would not last. The next minute he would smile at them, as Alfred remembered, "like the sun after a shower."

It was not surprising if Dickens sometimes felt the

house rather full of children. As for Kate, never energetic, she was always so busy nursing the next baby that she had no time for playing and dancing. As she grew older and plumper she was very glad to have her younger sister Georgina living with them to take many of the cares of children and household off her hands.

The main theme of *Bleak House* is the damage that people could suffer from being involved with the Court of Chancery, which at that time was slow-moving, sometimes took years to settle the inheritance of an estate, and showed small consideration for the Wards in Chancery placed under the care of the Court. Dickens had seen a good deal of these delays while he was working in the lawyer's office and reporting in Doctors' Commons. In *Bleak House* he attacked the Court of Chancery as representing "all authorities in all places and under all names whatsoever where false pretences are made, and injustice is done."

There are a great many characters in *Bleak House* and a variety of scenes ranging from the poor workman's cottage, to the great lord's mansion. They are all connected by the case of Jarndyce v. Jarndyce, which is delayed and postponed by the Court of Chancery over the whole period of the tale.

The story is told partly in the first person by Esther Summerson, partly in the third person whenever Dickens wanted to describe characters whom Esther did not know, and scenes at which she was not present.

Esther's birth is a mystery. She grows up first under the care of an unloving "Godmother," who always tells her that "Your mother is your disgrace and you were hers." When the aunt dies Esther is sent to school, though she does not know who keeps her there. Hungry for love after her arid childhood she soon finds it, for she herself has a kind and loving heart.

When she leaves school Esther finds that she is the protégée of a kindly, eccentric, middle-aged bachelor, John Jarndyce, who takes her to live at his home, Bleak House, so that she can keep house for him and for his two wards in Chancery, the cousins Ada and Richard.

There is an inheritance still to be decided, but John Jarndyce has had the strength of mind, and also enough money from other sources, to ignore the vague possibilities, and he is anxious to teach Ada and Richard to do the same. He wants Richard especially to adopt a profession, and to earn his own living without depending on his uncertain expectations.

There is an awful warning before them—"a curious little old woman in a squeezed bonnet" who haunts the Court of Chancery in hourly expectation of judgement in her favor which has never come. Poor old Miss Flite has long ago lost her wits in the sickness of hope deferred.

"Mad, young gentleman," she says to Richard, "I was a ward myself. I was not mad at that time, I had youth and hope. I believe beauty. It matters very little now. Neither of the three served or saved me. I have the honour to attend the court regularly. With my documents I expect a judgement shortly. On the Day of Judgement. I have discovered that the sixth seal men-

tioned in the Revelations is the Great Seal. It has been
open a long time!'"

Unfortunately Richard does not pay any attention to
the warning, and instead of working hard to make a living for himself and for Ada, who he loves, he eats his
heart out in expectation of the inheritance that never
comes.

Esther's story, the discovery of her mother's name,
and of the secret of her birth, is skillfully woven in and
out of the story of Richard and Ada. Miss Flite lodges in
a room above a sleazy shop and rag and bottle warehouse. Its owner is an evil old man named Krook, and
the shop is nicknamed The Chancery. It is Dickens'
image of the Court of Chancery and of the lawyers who
work there, while such poor half-crazed clients as Miss
Flite are represented by the rags and bottles.

An unknown man who lives by copying documents
for lawyers also lodges in Krook's house, and kills himself there. A great lady wrapped in her maid's cloak and
shawl comes secretly by night to find out from Jo, the
boy who sweeps the crossing nearby, how the unknown
man died and where he is buried.

Two people are trying to uncover the secret connected with Esther's birth: Mr. Tulkingham, Sir Lester
Deadlock's solicitor and man of business, who suspects
the proud and beautiful Lady Deadlock of a hidden past;
and Mr. Guppy, a clerk in the office of John Jarndyce's
lawyer, Kenge, who falls in love with Esther Summerson
at first sight, much to her displeasure since she does not

return his feelings. Mr. Guppy, who won't be discouraged, is seized by the idea that if he can discover the secret of Esther's birth and parentage she will be so grateful that she will marry him. He starts on some detective work of his own.

Esther is another of Dickens' too meek and unselfish girls, but she tells her story well, and binds together the various threads. She is stricken with smallpox half way through the book and loses her beauty, but her sweetness and thoughtfulness for all around her make her just as much loved, even by the man of all others whose love she has longed for without expecting it.

There are, as always, an amazing gallery of minor characters, most of them connected in some way with the Court of Chancery Mr. Krook's house alone provides more than one macabre story; Lady Deadlock's French maid has her part to play. The housekeeper at Deadlock Hall, Mrs. Rouncewell, almost certainly a portrait of Dickens' own grandmother, has two sons, a successful iron-founder in the North of England, and a roving ex-soldier; she also has a pretty granddaughter to contribute to the closely woven tapestry of human lives.

Dickens drew in Harold Skimpole, the light-hearted, charming, improvident, grown up "child" who lives mostly on other people, what was intended to be a portrait of the well-known editor, Leigh Hunt. The portrait, as so often when Dickens drew from a real person, must be a caricature of a part of Leigh Hunt. The editor who earlier recognized the quality of Keats from one line of his poetry and who was the friend of Byron and Shelley was much more of a person than Harold Skimpole.

Dickens was proud of the portrait and boasted of it, though he managed somehow to appease Hunt by vigorously denying that it was a whole representation of him.

Bleak House is a whole world of the imagination, permeated as always by the author's sympathy for the exploited, and anger against the exploiters. Drama is provided by the unfolding of the story of Esther's birth and parentage. There is not a page in the long novel that is not rich with observation and feeling, not a character who does not live. The book, though often relieved by humor and by Esther's happiness, which even disfigurement cannot destroy, is somber, and embraces as many facets of life as the names of Miss Flite's caged birds: "Hope, Joy, Youth, Peace, Rest, Life, Dust, Ashes, Waste, Want, Ruin, Despair, Madness, Death, Cunning, Folly, Words, Wigs, Rags, Sheepskin, Plunder, Precedent, Jargon, Gammon and Spinach."

Even while he was working on *Bleak House*, Dickens was also writing a *Child's History of England*. He had begun this with the idea of teaching history to his own children but the book, most of which he dictated to his sister-in-law, Georgina, was published serially in *Household Words* and soon afterward in volume form.

There is not very much to be said for it. It gives the the impression of having been hastily compiled from too little reading; it is full of prejudices and shallow judgements, and the writing is unworthy of the author. The *Child's History* only goes up to the year 1688, but there is a brief note at the end about the accession and marriage of Queen Victoria.

～(17)～

Dickens, always restless, was, during 1850–51, becoming impatient with John Forster. Forster was a valuable friend in many ways, but he was too possessive and domineering. He was jealous when Dickens made friends with a fellow novelist, Wilkie Collins. Collins was ten years younger than Dickens and had not yet published his most famous detective novels, *The Woman in White* and *The Moonstone*. He was deeply interested in the shape of his novels and in the construction of his plots. Dickens, who in his youth tumbled his riches carelessly into a book without paying much attention to the construction of the story, learned something from Wilkie Collins. He also very much enjoyed his company. As soon as *Bleak House* was finished Dickens and Collins went off together for a two-month vacation in Switzerland.

"Collins," Dickens wrote, "takes things easily and is

not put out by small matters, he eats and drinks everything, gets on well everywhere, and is always in good spirits." They both talked a lot of nonsense, argued and went about together or separately as they felt inclined. It was a kind of freedom Dickens did not enjoy at home, where there were now nine children, the latest a boy called Henry Fielding, nor did he enjoy it with John Forster, who was heavy handed and tried to manage him.

On his return Dickens gave a public reading from *The Christmas Carol* to help raise money for a new Literary and Scientific Institute in Birmingham. He had often read his books aloud to his friends by his own fireside, but this was the first time he had given a public reading from his works. It was an enormous success. At first Dickens was nervous, but soon he said, "We were all going on together as if we were sitting round the fire."

He was becoming very much concerned about the relationships of masters and men in industry. He saw that the mill owners and factory owners were making fortunes while the men who worked in the mills and mines were half-starved, and living in miserable houses hastily put up to make as much profit as possible when the towns were expanding rapidly after the introduction of machinery. "All things considered," Dickens wrote, "there never was a people so abused as the English at this time."

He made up his mind to write a novel about it, and started *Hard Times*.

He went up to Preston in Lancashire to get a first-hand impression of a strike. He arrived on a Saturday and was surprised to find the town looking so ordinary. The streets were empty, and since the weather was bitterly cold most people were indoors. The day after Dickens went to the meeting of strikers' delegates, and found none of the fierce demonstrations he had expected. He was impressed by the calmness and good sense of these men. The next day he looked on while the strike pay was distributed; then he went home.

But a little was always enough to set him going. He had seen enough of what was known as "a centre of manufacturing industry" to call it a "hell hole," and to draw the picture of Coketown, the scene of *Hard Times.*

Hard Times is shorter and more compact than any of Dickens' other novels. This may have been partly the result of the talks about construction with Wilkie Collins but it was also because Dickens wrote it for weekly serial publication instead of monthly. It is a somber book with almost none of his rich humor in it, but it is one of the most powerful things he ever wrote. He said that the ideas he wanted to express in it "took him by the throat."

There are two main ideas in *Hard Times.* One is that it is disastrous to educate children by teaching them only facts which may be useful to them when they grow up to earn their living. They need play, fun, stimulus to their imagination. Above all they need to respect human feelings more than money.

The circus with which *Hard Times* opens represents this side of life; the clowns and tumblers speak for freedom and gaiety and kindness. Mr. Bounderby, the suc-

He drew up a placard, offering twenty pounds reward for the apprehension of Stephen Blackpool. From Hard Times

cessful businessman in Coketown, the self-made man who has grown up with an eye only on profit and without regard for feeling and imagination, represents the other side of life.

Sissy Jupe, the circus child, who is adopted by Mr. Bounderby's friend, Mr. Gradgrind, is the only happy person in the book because the Gradgrinds and Bounderbys have caught her too late, she has already learned to love and feel. Gradgrind's children, Louisa and Tom, are ruined by their father's insistence on education only for money-making. Louisa makes a miserable marriage with Mr. Bounderby, because she has learned to distrust her instincts. When Tom is in trouble and disgrace, and his only hope is to flee the country, it is the circus people with their compassion and independence who save him.

Weaving in and out of this story is another theme, the relationship between master and men, in a world which had so recently been changed by the Industrial Revolution. Dickens, as is the way of genius, saw ahead of his time. His comment on the Preston strike was that the only solution for disputes between employers and employed was "Authorized Mediation." "Masters right or masters wrong," he wrote, "there is certain ruin to both in the continuance of frequent revivals of this breach."

Dickens finished *Hard Times* in six months. As he had hoped, it revived the falling circulation of *Household Words*. Reviewers did not like the book, which they accused of being "sullen socialism." Dickens was never sullen himself, but in this book he was writing mostly about sullen people, and it has none of the sparkle and color of his other novels.

Dickens was a socialist in the sense that, as he had said in his first public speech in the United States, he was for the Many against the Few, and that he believed that "nothing is high because it is in a high place, nothing is low because it is in a low one." But he never aligned himself with any political party, and he hated any avoidable interference by officialdom. He was for good feeling in public and private relationships, and for all who were oppressed against those who were oppressing them.

Love, the love of human beings for one another was the essence of his philosophy. Dickens was not a regular churchgoer, but he was a deeply religious man. He wrote to one of his sons:

"I now most solemnly impress on you the truth and beauty of the Christian religion, as it came from Christ himself, and the impossibility of your going wrong if you humbly and heartily respect it."

In his will Dickens urged his children to guide themselves by the teaching of the New Testament, which was the basis of his life and work.

Dickens at this time in his life was more and more drawn to France. In the summer of 1854 he took a villa at Boulogne and left two of the boys at school there. In February of the next year he went to Paris for a two weeks' vacation with Wilkie Collins, the friend whose company he now found most stimulating and enjoyable. In the summer of that year, 1855, Dickens brought his whole family over to Paris, to apartments in the Champs Elysées, where they stayed for seven months.

Dickens thought that the French had "more efficiency and purpose than the English." The administration of Paris seemed to him far more efficient than that of London. He had often said that the government of England was too much in the hands of one class, and he never got over his early impatience with the English Parliament. "It does so little and talks so much."

While in Paris he worked hard on his new novel, *Little Dorrit.* By now he spoke French fluently. He went often to the theater, his great pleasure in any city; he mixed with French writers and journalists. For a man of so much genius and such success he was extraordinarily free from vanity, but he did appreciate the greater respect shown to authors in France. It was perhaps the first time he had been with people who made him feel that his work would have lasting value as literature.

Since Dickens was still editing *Household Words* he had to go over to England once a month to compile the next issue of the magazine. This continual traveling suited his restless nature. The Dickens children were delighted to live on that splendid boulevard, where they saw everyone in Paris including the Emperor Napoleon III and the Empress Eugenie passing their windows. Dickens did not allow them to make a vacation of the visit; he arranged classes for them in French and Italian, and engaged a tutor. When he looked back at his own strenuous youth, and at the exertions that had made his fortune, he sometimes looked sadly at his "limp" sons, who seemed to have no particular ambition.

He himself devoured all the French books of the day, and especially admired the novels of Balzac, who had died just five years before, in 1850.

In spite of his enjoyment of Paris, in spite of hard work on *Little Dorrit*, and of the constant demands of *Household Words* across the Channel, Dickens was dissatisfied and restless. There was always something more that he wanted, something that he seemed to have lost and to be looking for. Perhaps it was something that had never existed outside his own imagination.

His disturbed state of mind was intensified by the reappearance of a figure out of his past. Maria Beadnell, now Mrs. Winter, suddenly wrote to her old admirer, Charles Dickens to say how much she would like to see him again. He answered her warmly; he had read her letter, "with a great emotion, and with an old tenderness, softened to a more sorrowful remembrance than I could easily tell you." He added, "the association my memory has with you invests it with a more immediate address to me that such a letter could have from anybody else. Mr. Winter will not mind that . . ."

Mr. Winter had no reason to feel jealous, for when the meeting took place Dickens was bitterly disillusioned. In his new novel *Little Dorrit* he introduces a character, Flora Finching, who was like Maria. He describes the feelings of Arthur Clennam, who had once been so much in love with her, on seeing her again. "Flora, always tall, had grown to be very broad too, but that was not much; Flora, whom he had left a lily had become a peony, but that was not much; Flora, who had seemed enchanting in all she said or thought was diffuse or silly, that was much. Flora, who had been spoiled and artless long ago, was determined to be spoiled and artless now. That was a fatal blow."

Little Dorrit opens in Marseilles, where several of the characters are in quarantine after returning from the East. Two men who later on play important parts in the story, the villainous Frenchman, Blandois, and the harmless little Italian, Cavaletto, are in prison there. After this opening the scene changes to London. *Little Dorrit* is divided into two parts, one called *Poverty*, the other called *Riches*.

There are several themes in the novel woven together into a complex pattern, so complex that for the first time Dickens put down on paper a plan of how the story worked out.

One theme is the story of the Dorrit family. William Dorrit has lived for so long in the debtors' prison that he is known as the Father of the Marshalsea. New arrivals are introduced to him, and it has become the custom for liberated debtors going out of the prison to present him with some parting token in money or kind. William's elder daughter, Fanny and his son, Tip, live outside the prison, where Fanny earns her living by dancing in the theater, in the chorus, and Tip in several dubious ways. William's brother Fred, an old clarinetist, also lives near the prison gates.

The younger Dorrit girl, Amy, born in the Marshalsea, lives there with her father, and earns money for his needs and her own by going out to do sewing and dressmaking in any house where she can find employment. She is entirely devoted to her pompous, selfish old father, who is to her a tragic and dearly loved figure.

Little Dorrit herself is the representative of love in the dark story rather than an individual human being. She is one of Dickens' meek, colorless young women without a thought for herself. She never for one instant loses patience with her tiresome father, and Fanny and Tip are glad to leave to her the whole burden of supporting and looking after him.

One of the places where Little Dorrit goes to work

is an old house in the city of London where the half paralyzed Mrs. Clennam sits brooding over ancient wrongs, and carrying on some kind of export business with the help of Joseph Flintwich, a cranky old servant. His bullied wife, Affery, terrified of "those two clever ones" looks after them.

The son of the house, Arthur Clennam, who has been abroad for years managing the foreign end of the business, returns to the gloomy house, where he had lived a shadowed childhood where mysteries seem to lurk. He notices Little Dorrit, quietly working in the background for Mrs. Clennam. He becomes so much interested in her that he traces her to her home in the Marshalsea, and does everything he can to befriend her. Thus Little Dorrit becomes the link between the story of her family and the story of the Clennams.

She also goes to sew for Arthur's early love, Flora, now the widow of a Mr. Finching. Flora lives in the house of her father, Mr. Casny, known from his misleading appearance of benevolence as, The Patriarch. His household is completed by a formidable old lady known as Mr. F's Aunt, whose occasional appearances are pure comedy, while Flora herself with her inconsequent chatter, her middle-aged flirtatiousness, and her warm genuine kindness, is for all her silliness one of the most attractive people in the novel.

Arthur Clennam, while in quarantine at Marseilles, made friends with Mr. Meagles, a retired banker, who was traveling with his wife, his pretty daughter, Pet, and Tattycoram, the orphan whom he had adopted to be a maid to Pet, and who sullenly resents the difference in station and prospects between herself and her young mistress. What happens to Pet and to Tattycoram makes another story linked to the other two by the friendship between the Meagles and Arthur Clennam.

All these stories have connections with Bleeding Heart Yard, a huddle of tumble-down houses in the city inhabited by very poor people. Here the hard-working and independent Daniel Doyce has a small factory where he perfects the inventions for which so far he can get no recognition; here lives Plornish, the carpenter, who, while serving a term in the Marshalsea, became a friend of Little Dorrit, and who now finds work for her by recommending her as a needle woman in the houses were he is employed. Here comes the Italian Cavaletto to lodge under Clennam's protection. Not far from the entrance to Bleeding Heart Yard is the tobacconist shop kept by the family of John Chivery, one of the Turnkeys at the Marshalsea, whose son young John Chivery is hopelessly in love with Little Dorrit. Pancks, the agent of Casby, collects the rents from the poor tenants of Bleeding Heart Yard.

Pancks plays an important part in the Dorrit story, for it is he who discovers that William Dorrit is really the heir to a large fortune of which he has known nothing. The father of the Marshalsea leaves the Marshalsea and travels luxuriously around Europe with Fanny and Tip, who are delighted with their new position, and with Amy, now very much in love with Arthur Clennam, who half regrets the old days in the Marshalsea when

she was Little Dorrit, and who is too unused to consid-
ering herself, and too unworldly to be able to derive
much pleasure from the new luxurious life.

Bleeding Heart Yard, drawn with great sympathy and
gentle humor, is the picture of extreme poverty in the
book. The Dorrits' new wealth brings them into contact
with the wealthiest people in the country. Mr. Merdles,
the financier, gray, dry, and dyspeptic, wanders like a
ghost through the lavish parties organized by his showy,
heartless wife. In Italy the Dorrits also encounter Pet, her
cynical, unkind husband, and Blandois, who has wormed
his way into their household.

Heartlessness is always for Dickens the worst sin, as
the loving heart is the first virtue. Although Little Dorrit
is a trying girl in some ways to the modern reader, she
does stand out against such people as the Merdles, Henry
Gowan, and Blandois, because of her capacity for loving.
We may be impatient with Little Dorrit but we are on
her side.

Heartlessness again is the fault of the Barnacles, the
large family with many ramifications, who are supposed
to represent the then governing class in England and the
civil service. The composite Ministry where they work
is called "The Circumlocution Office," whose sole object
is "not to get anything done." Young Barnacles, entering
this service, learn from the older ones how to prevent
anyone from doing anything.

Arthur Clennam goes to the Circumlocution Office in
the early part of the book to try and find out about
William Dorrit's debts in hopes of setting him free.

Doyce goes to try and patent his inventions. Neither application is successful. The Barnacles only care for getting or making jobs for themselves and their families and for delaying any other kind of action. Dickens is furious with them because they do nothing for such places as Bleeding Heart Yard while they dine luxuriously at the Merdles.

Dickens' satire is always partly based on prejudice. Much of what he drew was really there in the government of the country, but he ignored any other side to the question. His method was the same when he drew a character from real life; he took one facet of a character and enlarged it into a whole. His truth was always true but it was often a lopsided truth. It was always entertaining.

The various threads in the pattern are drawn together near the end of the novel. The financial crash and suicide of Merdles affects most of the characters, including those who live in Bleeding Heart Yard. The mystery of Mrs. Clennam's household, in which Blandois has become involved, explains itself: Little Dorrit's longing to love and be loved is at last fully satisfied.

Except for some of Flora's chatter and for the occasional glimpses of Mr. F's aunt, *Little Dorrit* does not contain much of Dickens' usual comedy, but it has the most crowded canvas, and the widest range of all his novels. As always the book is full of minor characters, each one acutely observed, skillfully presented, and completely alive. *Little Dorrit*, a world within the covers of a book, is one of the most mature works of this great master.

⊸ 18 ⊷

W<small>HILE</small> Dickens was still writing *Little Dorrit* he was also busy producing a play by Wilkie Collins called *The Frozen Deep*. It was a melodrama inspired by the accounts of Sir John Franklin's last Arctic expedition in search of the Northwest Passage. The two main characters in *The Frozen Deep* were the officers from two ships, Richard Wardour and Frank Aldersley, who, at home in England, had fallen in love with the same girl, Clara, who favored Aldersley. When the two men were marooned on an ice floe, Wardour, the stronger of the two, could have escaped alone, but for Clara's sake he stayed with Aldersley and kept him alive by sacrificing most of his own share of their food and coverings.

Dickens, who had helped to write the play, acted the part of Wardour with tremendous gusto, even growing a beard for it. One room in his house in Tavistock Square was converted into a theater. Young Charles Dickens, now nineteen, remembered that autumn was "one long rehearsal."

Dickens was in heaven, but managed somehow to write *Little Dorrit*, in the middle of all the confusion.

"Your aged friend," he wrote to Macready, "glides away on the Dorrit stream, forgetting the uproar for a stretch of hours, refreshing himself with a ten or twelve miles walk, pitches headforemost into foaming rehearsals, placidly emerges for editorial purposes, smokes over buckets of distemper, again calmly floats upon the Dorrit waters."

Meanwhile most of the amateur company camped out in the house for the whole day if not for the night as well. The expense of providing meals for them was enormous, and Kate had to go to the country for a week's rest cure. Georgina Hogarth and Dickens' two daughters, Mamey and Katie, played the female parts, and Forster read a prologue which Dickens wrote. There were four performances of *The Frozen Deep* and in each of them, when Dickens as Richard Wardour made his final speech blessing the lovers, and then died of exhaustion just under the Union Jack, the whole Victorian audience burst into tears.

Perhaps Dickens found the house in Tavistock Place dull after the theater had been dismantled, for in February of the following year, 1857, he realized one of his earliest ambitions. He bought Gad's Hill, the big house in the country near Rochester, which he had first seen when as a little boy he walked around the grounds with his father.

Dickens' House, Gad's Hill

He wrote to Angela Coutts to describe his new house.
"It is old fashioned, plain and comfortable. On the
summit of Gad's Hill with a noble prospect at the side
and behind looking down into the valley of the Medway.
Lord Darnley's Park at Cobham, (a beautiful place with
a noble walk through a wood) is close by. . . . It is
only an hour and a quarter from London by the Railway. To crown all (the inn) with the sign of Sir John
Falstaff is over the way and I used to look at it as a

wonderful mansion when I was a very little, odd child with the first shadows of all my books in my head, I suppose."

It was here that Dickens wrote all his later novels. Here his friends came to stay with him, arriving by train at Higham Station where they were met by a scarlet jaunting car, or by a basket-carriage drawn by a pony whose harness jingled with bells.

Here as soon as they had moved in Dickens finished writing *Little Dorrit*.

The first of their distinguished guests was the famous Danish writer of fairy tales for children, Hans Christian Andersen. He and Dickens had met before, and had always read and admired each other's work. Now Andersen spent five weeks at Gad's Hill, on excellent terms with his host and hostess and with their family of children, with whom he played games in the large field of clover near the house.

"The sons and I often lying there," he wrote. "There is a fragrance of clover, the elder tree is in blossom and the wild roses have an odour of apples so fresh and strong."

In the evening they would all walk up to the top of Gad's Hill, to watch the sun go down; to look at the smoke curling up from the cottages, and at the ships on the river Medway. They listened to the distant sound of church bells from the villages and to the nearby chirping of grasshoppers; while Dickens handed around a great bowl of claret cup with freshly picked borage floating on top.

In the end Dickens was relieved to see his guest leave, for Andersen was so devoted to his host that he wanted to spend the whole day talking to him, and Dickens had to work. Besides he was not the man to spend weeks quietly talking to one person. He wanted to rush back to the London house whenever he felt like it, and to go around seeing his other friends.

Soon after Andersen's departure, Dickens' second son, Walter Landor, went off to India to a post as cadet in the service of the East India Company. He never returned to England, the climate of India ruined his health and he died six years later.

One reason why Dickens was glad to have a country house as well as a town house was that he and his wife were getting on each other's nerves. Kate was worn out by her husband's restless activity and exuberance, and by the crowds of people he always had around him. He was impatient with her slowness and lack of interest in life. He had no doubt really been deeply disturbed by meeting Maria Beadnell Winter. She could be nothing to him now but she brought back the memory of the romantic love he had once felt, and of his hopes of glowing happiness, in a love which had never been realized.

The amateur company gave a very successful performance of *The Frozen Deep* before Queen Victoria, the Prince Consort and the King of the Belgians. Growing more and more ambitious, Dickens proposed to give performances in theaters in the North of England to raise funds for the widow of his friend, Douglas Jerrold.

A theater in Manchester booked the company for a performance. The stage here was too large for the voices and amateur accomplishments of Georgina, Mamey, and Katie, so Dickens engaged three professional actresses, Mrs. Ternan and her two daughters, Maria and Ellen. The performance was a huge success, and Dickens, who had never in his own estimation acted better, brought the house down.

The Manchester performance finally wrecked his disintegrating marriage. He had fallen in love with Ellen Ternan, a pretty, lively girl with fair hair, and large blue eyes, who adored the great author, who was also such a marvelous actor! Kate Dickens demanded a separation, and the household broke up. The sons went with their mother; the two daughters Mamey and Katie stayed with their father, and so did Georgina Hogarth, a disloyalty to her sister which shocked everybody.

The separation divided Dickens' friends. Angela Burdett Coutts would have no more to do with him, Thackery sided with Kate, and soon afterward quarreled with Dickens over the election of a mutual acquaintance to the Garrick Club.

A house was found for Kate in Gloucester Terrace. Dickens bought another house for Ellen Ternan in Peckham, then a country district of London. It was here that she is said to have borne him a son who died in infancy.

"I hope," wrote the gentle Kate, "to resign myself to God's will, and to lead a contented if not a happy life. My position is a sad one. Time only can blunt the keen pain I feel in my heart."

~(19)~

DICKENS, in a general state of upheaval, now quarreled with his publishers, Bradbury and Evans, who were also the publishers of the magazine *Household Words*. Dickens was so angry with them that he decided to start a new magazine of his own to beat *Household Words* out of the field. He knew that he would be well able to do this so long as it was he who wrote the serials for it. He wanted to call it *Household Harmony*, but his friends managed to convince him that this was hardly the moment for such a title. In the end he decided on *All The Year Round*. He announced that the first number would appear on April 30, 1859, and would contain the first installment of a new novel which he would write.

The novel was *A Tale of Two Cities*, a story of the French Revolution. *All The Year Round* was to be a weekly magazine, which meant that Dickens had to write shorter installments, as he had done with *Hard Times*.

He had found that the "small portions" drove him frantic then, and he found it now. He therefore aimed at writing a picturesque story full of action. His desire was that the characters should express themselves mostly by action, rather than as was more usual with him, by dialogue.

In spite of these limitations *A Tale of Two Cities* is a splendid historical novel, finely constructed, vivid and dramatic. Dickens explained in his preface that it was to be "a popular and picturesque means of understanding that great time though no one can hope to add anything to the philosophy of Mr. Carlyle's great book (Carlyle's *French Revolution*, a work which Dickens had always fervently admired). The theme was that oppression must always lead to anarchy, and anarchy to self destruction. *A Tale of Two Cities* expresses in a swiftly moving narrative all Dickens' feeling for the oppressed, first for the poor peasants of France starving and brutalized under the indifferent rule of the Crown and the heartless tyranny of the aristocracy; then for the aristocrats, imprisoned and sent in hundreds to the guillotine by the revengeful fury of the mob, and all those suspected of supporting them.

The central figure in the book is Lucie Manette, a French girl who as a child had been brought out of France when her father, a doctor, and was swept into the Bastille prison. Lucie had been educated in England, without any knowledge of her parentage.

Three men are grouped around Lucie. Her father, Doctor Manette, released, "recalled to life" after the storming of the Bastille in 1789 and reunited in England with his daughter; Charles Darnay, born Evrémonde, a young French emigré, who detests his family's attitude toward the peasants on their estates, and on his arrival in England changes his name from Evrémonde to Darnay, and sets out to earn his living in his adopted country. The third of the men in Lucie's life is Sidney Carton, a young lawyer of keen wits and great possibilities, which he drowns in drink, and in a cynical despair which prevents him from attempting to salvage his disordered life, but which does not prevent him from loving Lucie with a disinterested love, even after she has become the happy wife of Charles Darnay. There is a strong physical likeness between Darnay and Carton, which is one of the pivots of the story.

The framework that holds the story together is Tellson's Bank in London which also has a French branch, and many French connections, so that when the Revolution starts in Paris the London House of Tellson becomes a center for the emigrés, and the House of Tellson in Paris struggles to keep some sort of order in their affairs. Mr. Lorry, an experienced banker and kindly old bachelor, who first brought Lucie to England as a child, and remains her friend and protector, is a link between the two cities, and between all the characters. Jerry Croncher, the bank messenger, secretly a resurrectionist who digs us dead bodies by night and sells them to anatomists, is attached to Mr. Lorry as his servant when he travels on the affairs of Tellson's Bank.

All these people live in London in the first half of the

book: fate takes them all across the channel to the chaos of Paris during the reign of terror. Here Jerry Croncher, with his secret and sinister graveyard knowledge, plays a clinching rôle in the plot, and Sidney Carton, sacrificing himself to save Charles Darnay for the sake of Lucie, "a life for the life you love," redeems his own self-frustrating life by a heroic end. "It is a far far better thing I do now than I have ever done." There is an echo here of *The Frozen Deep*.

A Tale of Two Cities, the second of Dickens' two historical novels, is, like *Barnaby Rudge*, concerned with the uprising of a mob, and the terrors of existence in a city under their savage and capricious power. It is a far greater book than *Barnaby Rudge*. The story is so well and firmly knit that it is like a movement of destiny. The fortunes of the Manettes and the Evrémondes, joined in the present by the marriage of Charles and Lucie, are affected by the past, as Charles is first acquitted before the revolutionary Tribunal in Paris on the evidence of the old Doctor who had suffered so bitterly at the hand of the Evrémondes and is then freshly accused on the evidence of the paper accusing the Evrémondes which Doctor Manette had written and hidden years ago in his room in the Bastille.

Each side is personified by a relentless figure, the old Marquis of Evrémonde, who could run over a poor child in the streets of Paris without a qualm, who sent Doctor Manette to the Bastille, is not more formidable than Madame Defarge, one of the blood drunk tricoteuses of revolutionary Paris, who pursues her private vengeance

After the sentence. From A Tale of Two Cities

against the Evrémonde family until she is foiled by Sidney Carton and is killed by Lucie's old nurse Miss Pross. Old Evrémonde and Madame Defarge are figures of hate, but it is the figures of love, Sidney Carton and Miss Pross, to both of whom Lucie matters more than their own lives, who win in the end.

A Tale of Two Cities was much admired by all Dickens' friends except Wilkie Collins who hinted that he could have worked out the plot better. Dickens retorted that "if it had been done in your manner it would have been overdone, too elaborately trapped, baited and prepared." The point was not to arouse suspense but to design a pattern of personal relationships, affected by a great historical event, and "to show by a backward light" Dickens said, "what everything had been working to."

The sales of *All The Year Round* shot up with the first installment of *A Tale of Two Cities*. Dickens' eldest son Charles now worked in the office of *All The Year Round*, which he was to inherit after his father's death. The third Dickens boy, Francis, also worked on the magazine for a time, while trying to make up his mind what he wanted to do. *All The Year Round* was a great success and money flowed in. As soon as he had finished *A Tale of Two Cities* the tireless Dickens began to write a series of articles for the magazine, which were outlined in a book called the *Uncommercial Traveller*. He varied this desk work by a fresh series of public readings.

Dickens now lived mostly at Gad's Hill with his two daughters, and his sister-in-law Georgina, who kept house for them. Mamie, the elder girl, was so devoted to her father and so much under Georgina's thumb that she accepted the situation calmly and would have nothing to do with her mother. Katie, the younger daughter, was unhappy, went to see her mother at regular intervals, and soon became engaged to Charles, brother of Wilkie Collins. Dickens himself overlooked all the details of the housekeeping. He had a passion for punctuality and tidiness. He insisted on meals being ready on time, and he went around the house at least once a day to see that everything was in order.

He could not sit down to work happily if one of the ornaments on his writing table was out of place. On it he kept a pair of bronze frogs, a rabbit on a gilt leaf, an ivory paper knife, a model of a man with puppies in his pockets, and a green cup which, whenever possible, was always full of fresh flowers. If any of these had been moved by so much as an inch he found it distracting. Sometimes he made a sortie from his work to see if all the croquet hoops and cricket stumps had been put away in the garden, or if the coats and hats of the boys were hanging on the pegs allotted to them.

Perhaps his sons found all this fussing difficult. Probably they were swamped by the sheer vitality, the restless energy, and the fame and success of their father. Dickens was worried because they seemed to him lacking in drive and purpose, and they were slow in getting on their own feet. Charley worked on *All The Year Round*, and Walter had to be shipped off to India; Francis, who thought he would like to be a doctor, had such a serious stammer that he was obliged to give up the idea. He thought of farming abroad and suggested that he could do very well if his father would start him with "Fifteen pounds, a horse and a rifle." But, Dickens said, he would be robbed of the fifteen pounds, the horse would throw him, and the rifle would blow his head off. In the end, Francis, after working for a while in the office of *All The Year Round*, went off to join the Bengal Mounted Police. He died in Canada at forty-two years old.

Alfred D'Orsay Tennyson, and Edward Bulwer Lytton, after trying various things unsuccessfully—perhaps their names were too much for them—went off to Australia. Henry Fielding was the most promising of the boys. He won a scholarship to Trinity College, Cambridge. He stayed in England, was knighted, and died in 1913.

When Dickens left home it was generally to give those public readings from his own books which were becoming more and more popular, and his performances, with which he took a great deal of trouble, grew better and better.

Dickens did not so much read as act every part.

"I had no conception before hearing Dickens read," Thomas Carlyle wrote, "of what capacities lie in the human face and voice. No theatre stage could have had more players than seemed to flit about his face, and all tones were present; there was no need of any orchestra."

Dickens read in all the big cities of England, Scotland and Ireland. In every place thousands of people were turned away from the door. Sometimes the audience went on cheering long after he had finished bowing to them from the stage, and had changed his coat behind the scenes and left the building. His own favorite reading was from *David Copperfield*. He worked for weeks to make a condensed story out of this, his best loved book. Of course he himself enjoyed the readings enormously. He had always half wanted to be an actor. "It is a great sensation to have an audience in one's hand," he said.

More than once his control of an audience saved a

theater full of people. One evening in a London theater
the drapery on the stage caught fire. The audience began
to rush toward the only exit, but Dickens shouted, "Sit
down, every one of you!" and, as if hypnotized, the
whole audience obeyed him. He called over his shoulder
to the stagehands to put out the fire, and went on with
the scene.

Once in Newcastle a gas batten fell with a crash and
started a stampede. A woman in the stalls screamed and
ran toward Dickens, who said laughingly, "There's nothing the matter, I assure you, pray sit down." There was
a real danger of a big fire, and the men who went to
restore the batten were terrified. One of them said afterward, "There stood the master as cool as ever I seen
him a-lounging at a railway station . . . The more you
want of the master the more you'll find in him."

In September 1860, when he had just been reading the
biography of some famous man, Dickens decided to destroy as much of his own past as possible. He made a
bonfire in the grounds of Gad's Hill of the letters he had
kept. This unfortunately meant that he destroyed letters
from Carlyle, Tennyson, Browning, Thackeray and
Wilkie Collins, but of course the letters that he himself
had written remained in the hands of his correspond-
ents, and many of them have since been published, the
most complete collection in the Nonesuch Edition, in
London 1937–8.

But even the intoxicating pleasures of public readings
had to give way to writing. *All The Year Round* was
running a serial by a writer named Charles Lever and

the sales were dropping. A new serial by Dickens was needed to pull them up again. He set himself to look for an idea, and found one, originally intended for an article, which he soon expanded into the design for the novel *Great Expectations*.

Forster had complained that there was not much of Dickens' comedy in *A Tale of Two Cities*. Dickens wrote to Forster that "you will not have to complain of the want of humour in *Great Expectations*."

Great Expectations is, like *David Copperfield*, the story of the first half of a man's life told in the first person. Pip, like David, is at the start a sensitive and vulnerable small boy at the mercy of older people. In Pip's life harshness comes from the older sister who has "brought him up by hand," often a heavy hand, and doesn't intend that Pip or anybody else should forget it. Gentleness comes from her husband, Joe Gargery, who gives to the orphan child in his home a father's patient and enduring love.

Two unexpected characters break the even tenor of Pip's childhood. Magwitch, an escaped convict, seizes the terrified child as he is wandering on the marsh and forces him to bring him food and a file to use on his leg irons. Magwitch is soon afterward recaptured, but hastily covers Pip by saying that he himself had stolen the file and the food.

The other macabre character is Miss Haversham, who, having been jilted on her wedding day, has lived ever since in the clothes that she had put on for the wedding with the preparations for the feast, even to the now rotted wedding cake on the table. She has with her a beautiful scornful little girl, Estella, who makes fun of Pip for having coarse hands, thick boots, and rough speech. This arouses in him a furious desire for refinement, and a new tendency to tell lies, though Joe says to him, "If you can't get to be uncommon through going straight, you'll never get to do it through going crooked."

But Pip yearns for anything that will make Estella love him instead of despising him. When a very young man, he is suddenly told by a lawyer that an unknown patron is going to leave him a handsome property, and is in the meantime going to give him a large enough allowance for him to finish his education and learn to live like a gentleman, Pip's first thought is that this will bring him nearer to Estella. He believes that his nameless benefactor is Miss Haversham who must, he thinks, have arranged this for him so that he can become a worthy suitor for the girl he has so often met in her house.

Pip lives in London, going to a tutor, learning to be a man about town and sharing an apartment with his tutor's son, Herbert Pocket, who has true refinement and delicacy, based on integrity and imaginative concern for other people, which Pip, now ashamed even of Joe, has not yet achieved.

Pip still tries to win Estella, still believes that his new life with its opening horizons is based on Miss Haversham's bounty. At this stage he is, perhaps not unnaturally, a confused young snob, altogether too muddled up about real quality to appreciate the fact that he has abandoned it in Joe.

Reality breaks through with the shock of discovering that his real benefactor is not Miss Haversham but Magwitch, the convict whom he had tried to help on the marsh. Magwitch, having made a fortune in Australia, determined to devote it to "making a gentleman" of the little boy who lingered in his mind as the last person in his own country who had shown him any kindness.

Pip, at first shattered by finding out that he owes his good fortune to a convict, is broken-hearted by Estella's marriage to another man. He loses another illusion as he discovers that Miss Haversham, far from helping him with his courtship of Estella, has always designed the girl to work out her own revengeful fury for her by making men unhappy. When he learns that Estella is the daughter of Magwitch and of a woman tried for murder, Pip has to part with the last of his dreams.

In this dark period of his life he learns to feel true gratitude and affection for the old convict who has done so much for him. He learns the full value of the faithful love that Joe has always given him, and comes to forget himself in the last cares for the dying Magwitch.

Estella's husband dies, and Pip later on has an unexpected meeting with her among the ruins of part of Miss Haversham's house which has been destroyed by a fire that killed her.

Dickens originally meant Pip and Estella to part forever at this last meeting, but Forster and other friends objected so strenuously that for once he distrusted his own instincts, and wrote another ending which concluded, "I saw no shadow of another parting from her."

It was a mistake for the whole trend of the novel is toward the breakdown of false hopes, and the original ending was more in keeping.

Great Expectations is a novel about disillusionment and the exchange of false values for true ones but it is illuminated as Dickens promised by his old humor. There are some wonderful comic characters, Mr. Pumplechook a village worldling and time server; the briefly sketched but amusing "Trabbs boy: Wemmer the Lawyer's Clerk with his sunset gun mounted on the roof of his small suburban house." But apart from these the whole book is shot through with irony, though this does not detract from the sympathy with which the reader sees poor Pip stumbling about in his half fantasy world.

Great Expectations is magnificently constructed and finely written, in what the modern English novelist, Graham Greene, calls "the secret prose" of Dickens' later books, which gives the reader, "the sense of a mind speaking to itself when there is no one there to listen." "The work has been pretty close," Dickens wrote, "but I hope the book is a good book." The novelist Bulwer Lytton wrote to him, "I am deep in the back numbers of your tale. What freshness and gusto! I know of none of yours more enchanting."

～ 21 ～

As soon as Dickens had finished *Great Expectations*, he went to Paris to give a series of readings from his books.

"The reading so stuns and oversets the Parisians," he wrote, "that I shall have to do it again. Blazes of Triumph!"

The readings were becoming one of the most important things in his life. They satisfied his old longing to appear on the stage, and he enjoyed actually seeing and hearing proof of his enormous popularity with his readers. The remarkable thing is that with all his success and popularity he always remained natural and unpretentious.

He had finished *Great Expectations* at the end of 1862. He spent a year mostly giving readings in France and England, but he also wrote one of his best Christmas stories, *Mrs. Lirriper's Lodging*.

There were happy times at Gad's Hill; Christmas was still the great festivity it had always been to Dickens. The house would be so full of guests that half of them would have to be boarded out at the Falstaff Inn nearby. On Christmas Day they would all sit around the large mahogany table in the dining room at Gad's Hill, the walls behind them wreathed with holly and ivy. As the Christmas pudding, bright with flaming brandy, was carried in Dickens would rise to give his favorite toast.

"Here's to us all, God Bless Us." At these Christmas parties he would be the gay, stimulating host he had always been, and would take a week off work to look after his guests. He worked now in a chalet, the gift of a Swiss author, which had been set up in the garden at Gad's Hill at a little distance from the house so that Dickens could be completely undisturbed while writing.

But in between the parties and the visits of guests he was more and more depressed. He was probably never really quite happy about the break-up of his marriage. Not much is known of his association with Ellen Ternan, but it seems from what we do know that he did not find great happiness with her. He was growing tired, and his longing for some satisfaction, he did not know what, grew stronger. He himself wrote that he was, "always looking for something" which he might possibly find, "a few thousand years hence in some other part of some other system, God knows." He began to feel that most men were unsatisfied by reality, they were all "instinctively unwilling to be restored to consciousness" when they awoke in the morning. Early in 1864 he started his last complete novel, *Our Mutual Friend*.

He found it very hard to begin. He was not feeling well and was depressed.

"I know from two days' slow experience," he wrote, "that I have a very mountain to climb before I see the open country of my work."

Feeling himself on the verge of a breakdown he took a vacation in France. On the way home from Dover to London he was involved in a terrible railway accident. The train in which he was traveling ran into a gap in the rails where the line was being repaired. Eight coaches were hurled over a bridge into the river below. Dickens' coach was just behind these; it "hung inexplicably suspended in the air over the side of the broken bridge."

Dickens, always calm in emergencies, said to the people sharing his compartment, "We can't help ourselves, but we can be calm and composed . . . Our danger must be over. Will you remain here without stirring while I get out of the window."

He climbed out of the window above the abyss, found one of the guards, got hold of two planks and extricated his companions. Afterward he worked for hours among the injured and dying.

He showed no signs of shock at the time, but for some days afterward he became sick and faint whenever he tried to write, and his nerves never fully recovered from the delayed shock. This added to his difficulties in writing the early chapters of *Our Mutual Friend*.

Our Mutual Friend opens with a sinister scene on London's river Thames as night is falling. Gaffer Hexham, a disreputable waterside character, who lives by what he can pick up out of the river, is in a boat rowed by his shrinking daughter, Lizzie. A dead body, secured by a rope trails in the water behind the boat, Hexham, as Lizzie sees with sorrow, slips into his own pocket the money he has taken from the pocket of the dead man. When they bring the body on shore it is identified as that of John Harmon, a young man who was returning from South Africa to take up a large inheritance bequeathed to him by his father.

This inheritance is the central theme of *Our Mutual Friend*. Old Harmon had made three wills, one leaving all his money to his son John on condition that he marry Bella Wilfer, a girl quite unknown to him who happened to have caught his father's fancy. The second will, which old Harmon had hidden and which is only discovered by chance in the course of the story, left all his wealth to the Crown; the third bequeathed the estate to the manager Noddy Boffin, who since young Harmon is reported drowned, and the second will is unknown, takes up the inheritance.

The estate, known as "the dust heaps" or "the mounds" is really a vast sewage farm. Mr. Boffin, and his wife, as simple, kind and honest a couple as ever lived, are sorry for Bella Wilfer, who has been so suddenly disappointed of a young husband and a rich marriage. They go to look for her and find her a pretty, spoiled, willful, charming girl. Dickens drew her from Ellen Ternan, and she has more character than most of his young women.

Bella goes to live with the Boffins for a time. To her

father whom she sincerely loves, she makes no secret of her determination to marry for money. She exclaims, "I love money, I want money, I want it dreadfully. I hate to be poor and we are degradingly poor, beastly poor."

The Wilfer family consists of Bella's father, Reginald Wilfer, known as Rumpty, or R.W., a gentle, affectionate, poorly paid clerk working in the City; Mrs. Wilfer, one of Dickens' old uproariously funny characters, and Bella's shrewish teenage sister, Lavinia or Livvy.

The Wilfers have a room to let, and a tenant offers himself, a young man with a reserved manner who produces no references except a quarter's pay in advance.

This young man, John Rokesmith, becomes secretary to Mr. Boffin, much to Bella's indignation, as she resents the connection with her own home, and suspects withdrawn Rokesmith of having some dire secret to hide.

Mrs. Boffin as a rich woman remains the same kind honest creature that she has always been, but Bella begins to think that riches are spoiling Mr. Boffin, who is always saying that everyone wants to get money out of him.

Bella is conscious of John Rokesmith's growing admiration, but rejects him angrily when he suddenly asks her to marry him. All the same she begins to love him as she sees how his integrity and selfless devotion to the Boffins' interests stand out against Mr. Boffin's new meanness and suspicion.

Mr. Boffin sacks Rokesmith in front of Bella for having dared to aspire to her hand when she is rightly reserving herself for a rich husband. Bella leaves all her fine new clothes and jewels behind and in the old dress she came in runs to her father where John Rokesmith joins her, and they declare their love for one another and soon afterward are married.

They live happily in a cottage where a baby girl is born to them. Then there is a sudden, and to Bella terrifying visit from the police, and an expedition to the riverside inn at the spot where Gaffer Hexham had brought ashore the body identified as John Harmon. Bella now discovers that it was the body of a man rather like John Harmon who had sailed on the same boat from the Cape and with whom John Harmon had exchanged clothes. Bella's husband is the John Harmon for whom she had been destined; he and Mr. Boffin have been testing her, and they are all reunited in happiness and begin to put the Harmon money to good use.

This is the main line of the novel, but as always with Dickens' later works, many other threads are woven into the pattern. There is the riverside life, the fortunes of Lizzie Hexham and of her younger brother, Charlie, who is so anxious to rise in the world that he is prepared to disown the sister who has been a mother to him. There is Mortimer Lightfoot, the young solicitor who handles the Harmon estate, and his friend Eugene Wrayburn, a briefless barrister, a cynical young man-about-town who crosses Lizzie Hexham's path. There is his rival with Lizzie, Bradley Hexham, a shoolmaster with furious passions raging under his respectable exterior.

Mortimer Lightfoot, dines half scornfully with the newly rich and snobbish Veneerings, who have a collection of dearest friends whom they hardly know, and who only visit them because they are rich; money in one way or another is the recurring theme in *Our Mutual Friend*. At the Veneerings Mortimer and Eugene meet Mr. Podsnap, who is a sharply pointed satire on all that was most complacent and materialistic in British middle class society in the mid-Victorian age.

"Mr. Podsnap was well to do and stood very high in Mr. Podsnap's opinion. Beginning with a good inheritance he had married a good inheritance, and had thrived exceedingly well in the Marine Insurance way, and was quite satisfied. He never could make out why everybody was not quite satisfied and he felt conscious that he set a brilliant social example in being particularly well satisfied with most things, and above all things himself."

The person who is not satisfied is his timid, plain young daughter, Georgina Podsnap, who looks outside her family for the affection and understanding she never had, and is deluded into believing that she finds it in two unscrupulous adventurers, Mr. and Mrs. Alfred Lammle. They again are connected with the gentle old Jew, Riah, whom Dickens probably intended as a contrast to his wicked old Jew, Fagin in *Oliver Twist*, and through him to the lame doll's dressmaker who is Lizzie Hexham's friend.

So the threads are bound together. Once again Dickens satirizes hypocrisy, complacency, and snobbery, which in this book is snobbery about money. Once again he presents in the Boffins, in Rumpty Wilfer, in Lizzie Hexham, in the doll's dressmaker and Riah, in Bella when her real self is liberated by love, the virtues of warmhearted simplicity, humanity and true humility which always come first with him.

Dickens said while he was writing *Our Mutual Friend*, "It is a combination of drollery with romance that requires a great deal of pains, and a perfect throwing away of points that might be amplified, but I hope it is very good. I confess in short I think it is."

Henry James, then a very young man, reviewing *Our Mutual Friend*, remarked that he had seldom read a book "so intensely written, so little seen and felt." To him the characters were "essentially small" but the *Times* critic after making some sharp criticism concluded, "Of Mr. Dickens' main story we cannot speak too highly. It is a masterpiece."

It was published as usual in monthly installments in *All The Year Round*. It was Dickens last complete novel.

~{ 22 }~

As soon as he had finished *Our Mutual Friend*, Dickens embarked on a new series of readings. He was now beginning to feel very ill; he suffered from a painful lameness in one foot, his heart was failing and he often felt faint after reading, but he would not cut short the tour. The readings paid very highly, and he was anxious to provide for his large family. None of his sons was doing very well, they seemed to have inherited something of the fecklessness of John Dickens rather than the driving energy of their father, and Charles Dickens had his wife and daughters to provide for, as well as Georgina, and Ellen Ternan. Also he enjoyed the readings enormously, and however ill he had been feeling during the day he always came to life again as soon as he stepped onto the platform.

His manager, Dolby, who accompanied him on this tour of England, left it on record that ill as Dickens felt he was, "always cheerful and good humoured when on tour, even in the most trying situations." He was still the most charming company, Dolby said that "he made the most ordinary things of life seem special in his presence."

Dickens now planned a reading tour in the United States, which would include Boston, New York, Baltimore and a few small cities in the East. In spite of the unpopularity that he had aroused after his first visit, his books, many of them now published by honest publishers on a proper business footing, were still widely read there, and there was a warm welcome awaiting him. Dickens was anxious to go again, and to meet the American people with a more mature understanding. He said at a farewell banquet in London that he so much wanted to renew his acquaintance with "a kind, large hearted, and generous people."

This time he was obliged to rest during the day when he was not traveling, and to cut social engagements to a minimum. Even so the tour was almost more than he could manage, though he never missed a reading.

"I am nearly used up," he wrote to Forster. "Climate, distance, catarrh, travelling and hard work. (I may say so now that they are nearly over) have begun to tell heavily on me."

According to Dolby who went with him, he never complained, never failed to give a good performance.

The New York press, no longer hostile, gave a farewell banquet to Dickens in New York, at which he thanked the American people for their warm welcome and said that throughout his tour he had "everywhere

Farewell to Dickens

been received with unsurpassable politeness, delicacy, sweet temper, hospitality and consideration." The reconciliation was complete.

The sea voyage made him feel much better for the time being, but when he landed in England his friends sadly saw a change in him. He seemed to have lost some of the elasticity of his bearing, and of the remarkable brightness of his eyes. His doctors advised him to give up the readings, but he took on another series of a hundred. These included a new reading, the murder scene from *Oliver Twist*, which had such an effect on the audience that dozens of women were carried out fainting. The dramatic effort of this scene exhausted Dickens, and after giving the final readings of the series in London in the early weeks of 1870 he told his audience that these were the very last. He intended in the future to give all his time to writing.

Since the Fall before he had been thinking of writing a mystery. Now he sat down at Gad's Hill to begin it. He had his usual difficulty in making a start, but he was able to supply *All The Year Round* with the first installment for the April number.

The novel was called *The Mystery of Edwin Drood.* Dickens did not live to finish it, and no one knows how he meant the story to work out. The scene is laid in Cloisterham, an imaginary cathedral town in the South of England. Jasper Drood, a man of twenty-nine who has spent his early life in the Far East, is first discovered in an opium den near the docks in London smoking pipes filled and supplied by a haggard woman who

clearly has had some earlier connection with him. Jasper comes back to Cloisterham, slips into the cathedral and hears the words "When the wicked man" intoned. Dickens said that this was the keynote of the story.

Jasper has a nephew Edwin Drood, of whom he seems very fond. Edwin is betrothed by an arrangement between their two fathers, now dead, to a young girl, Rosa Budd, who is still at school in Cloisterham. Jasper is obviously attracted by Rosa, and she as clearly is frightened of him.

One of the Canons attached to the cathedral, Septimus Crisparkle, who is as clear-hearted and lively as his name suggests, invites two young people, wards of a friend, to stay with him for a time to finish their education. Helena and Neville Landless are both dark, slenderly built and handsome. They, like Jasper, have spent some years in the Far East.

A quarrel springs up between Edwin Drood and Neville. Jasper asks them both to dinner with the declared purpose of helping with a reconciliation. Edwin Drood disappears that evening, and Neville is suspected of murdering him. But while these suspicions gather Edwin's guardian in London, Mr. Grewgious, is also making inquiries about his ward's disappearance. But the woman of the opium den and a mysterious character called Datchery come down to Cloisterham. Mr. Datchery is probably Grewgious' clerk, who was mentioned as being fond of amateur theatricals, but this can only be a guess, as we never learn who he is in the unfinished part of the book.

To add to the mystery there is an odd character called Stony Durdles, a stone mason, who is constantly exploring the old tombs of the cathedral by night and who allows Jasper to come with him on some of these expeditions. The trend of the story seems to suggest that Jasper had himself murdered Edwin Drood and had buried the body somewhere among these old tombs, but this we shall never know. The book includes the last of Dickens' marvelous comic characters, Mr. Sapsea the auctioneer, a pompous creature who models himself closely after the dean of the cathedral and always hopes to be mistaken for him.

Mr. Sapsea produces a wonderful epitaph for his wife which he wants Durdles to engrave on her monument.

ETHELINDA
Reverential wife of
Mr. Thomas Sapsea
Auctioneer, Valuer, Estate Agent
of this city.
Whose knowledge of the World,
Though somewhat extensive
Never brought him acquainted with
A Spirit,
More capable of
LOOKING UP TO HIM.
Stranger, pause,
And ask thyself the question.
CANST THOU DO LIKEWISE?
If not
WITH A BLUSH RETIRE.

What fun Dickens must have had writing that!

On June 8, 1870 he was at Gad's Hill, and wrote as usual all the morning. He generally finished work at lunch time, but on that day he went back to his desk after lunch. At dinner time, he complained of feeling very ill, and got up from the table only to fall on the floor in a seizure. He never regained consciousness, and died in the evening of the next day, June 9th.

Burial of Dickens in Westminster Abbey

He was buried in Westminster Abbey on July 14th while the whole nation mourned for him.

"As a charming companion I never knew his equal," wrote Charles Eliot Norton. "I never knew a famous and flattered man so utterly unhurt by it all . . . the better one knew him the more one loved him."

The famous scholar Benjamin Jowett, speaking at a memorial service for Dickens, said,

"He whose loss we now mourn occupied a greater space than any other writer in the minds of Englishmen during the last thirty-five years."

Charles Dickens

1812. Born at Landport, Portsmouth, on February 7th.

1817. Went to live at Chatham.

1823. Family removed to Camdem Town, London. Father imprisoned for debt in the Marshalsea.

1824. Went to work in Warren's Blacking Factory. Removed from Blacking Factory after his father's release from prison. Went to school at the Wellington Academy, London.

1827. Started work as office boy in a lawyer's office. Transferred to job as clerk in firm of Ellis and Blackmore, solicitors in Gray's Inn.

1829. Fell in love with Maria Beadnell. Began to learn shorthand.

1832. Joined staff of paper, *The True Sun,* as Parliamentary Reporter.

1833. Gave up hope of marrying Maria Beadnell.
First publication, Sketch called *Dinner at Poplar* in *Monthly Magazine.*

1834. Transferred to staff of *Morning Chronicle.*

1836. *Sketches by Boz* published.
First installment of *Pickwick Papers* published.
Married Catherine Hogarth (Kate).
Sept. Kate's younger sister, Mary Hogarth, came to live with them.
Nov. Dickens gave up reporting and began to edit Bentley's Magazine.

1837. First child born, and christened Charles.
Mary Hogarth died suddenly.
Moved to house in Doughty Street.
First installment of *Oliver Twist* published in Bentley's Magazine.
John Forster became Dickens' man of business.

1838. First installment of *Nicholas Nickleby* appeared in Bentley's Magazine.

1840. Dickens began to edit magazine called *Master Humphrey's Clock,* first installment of *The Old Curiosity Shop* appeared in it.

1842. First installment of *Barnaby Rudge* appeared in *Master Humphrey's Clock.*
First visit to America, January to June.
Published *American Notes.*

1843. First installment of *Martin Chuzzlewit* appeared.
Christmas Carol published.

1844. Went to live in Italy.
The Chimes published at Christmas.

1845. Returned to live in England, in Tavistock Square, London.

1846. Became Editor of the *Daily News* in January and resigned in February.

1847. First installment of *Dombey and Son* published.

1849. First installment of *David Copperfield* published.

1850. Dickens started editing new magazine called *Household Words*.
Produced plays for amateur company, and acted in them.

1852. First installment of *Bleak House* appeared in *Household Words*.

1853. First installment of *Hard Times* appeared in *Household Words*.

1856. First installment of *Little Dorrit* appeared in *Household Words*.

1858. Separated from his wife.
Bought a country house, Gad's Hill near Rochester.

1859. Broke with publishers of *Household Words* and started a new magazine of his own called *All The Year Round*.

1861. First installment of *Great Expectations* appeared in *All The Year Round*.
Dickens gave constant public readings from his works.

1864. Health began to fail. Continues with readings.

1865. Involved in railway accident at Staplehurst in Kent.

1866. Went to America for the second time for a

reading tour. Publication of First Installment of *Our Mutual Friend* in *All The Year Round*.

1869.   Gave last public readings.

1870.   First installment of *Edwin Drood* appeared in *All The Year Round*.

Dickens died at Gad's Hill on June 9th.

Buried in Westminster Abby, June 14th.